Aging
Gratefully

Aging Gratefully

A 30-Day Devotional for Women

Heather Creekmore

Our Daily Bread
Publishing.

Aging Gratefully: A 30-Day Devotional for Women
© 2024 by Heather Creekmore

Published in association with Books & Such Literary Management, 52 Mission Circle, Suite 122, PMB 170, Santa Rosa, CA 95409-5370, www.booksandsuch.com.

Requests for permission to quote from this book should be directed to: Permissions Department, Our Daily Bread Publishing, PO Box 3566, Grand Rapids, MI 49501, or contact us by email at permissionsdept@odb.org.

Interior design by Michael J. Williams

Library of Congress Cataloging-in-Publication Data

Names: Creekmore, Heather, 1974- author.
Title: Aging gratefully : a 30-day devotional for women / Heather Creekmore.
Description: Grand Rapids, MI : Our Daily Bread Publishing, [2024] | Summary: "With 30 devotional readings, Heather Creekmore invites women 45 to 65 to find delight in the Bible's perspective on aging, to embrace God's grace for living joyfully, and to thank God for the gift of getting older" -Provided by publisher.
Identifiers: LCCN 2023041720 (print) | LCCN 2023041721 (ebook) | ISBN 9781640702325 (paperback) | ISBN 9781640702370 (epub)
Subjects: LCSH: Christian women--Prayers and devotions. | Aging--Prayers and devotions. | Devotional calendars. | BISAC: RELIGION / Christian Living / Women's Interests | SELF-HELP / Aging
Classification: LCC BV4527 .C777 2024 (print) | LCC BV4527 (ebook) | DDC 242/.643--dc23/eng/20231023
LC record available at https://lccn.loc.gov/2023041720
LC ebook record available at https://lccn.loc.gov/2023041721

Printed in the United States of America
24 25 26 27 28 29 30 31 / 8 7 6 5 4 3 2 1

Contents

Introduction

On the game show *Supermarket Sweep*, contestants rush through the aisles of a grocery store with a checklist, tossing in items as they try to beat the clock. Their faces reveal the blend of stress and excitement that comes with racing to a big finish. My life has felt like that game show. I rushed through school, skipping my senior year of high school to go to college early. When I learned I could start working as an intern while finishing my bachelor's degree, I skipped out of college early too. Check the box. Move on. What's next on my list?

In my mid-twenties I landed my dream job—campaign manager. It was up to me to get my boss elected to Congress. I worked seventy hours a week. Even when I wasn't at work, my mind never left campaign mode. For eleven months I immersed myself in the political process. The morning after election day, I was unemployed. We'd lost. Game over.

A year of my life had been donated to a cause that evaporated the second the news channel declared a winner. I was untethered. What was I doing with my life?

I jumped to the next thing, then the next. I met my husband at thirty and thought the marriage milestone would free me to slow down and savor the years. But it didn't. By our fifth anniversary, we had four children aged four and under. My life goal changed from finding the next career opportunity to getting babies to sleep through the night. As soon as this one could walk or this one could buckle his own car seat, then I'd be able to rest.

But as every mother knows, rest doesn't come when you stop buying diapers. As the kids progressed into tweens and teens, my drive to get on to the next season of life and my desire to stop the clock became constant competitors. Now, as I watch my children continue to age, I'm reminded daily of how I am aging too. I've suddenly surged into a new stage—midlife. Some days I'm still racing so hard, I don't recognize it or stop to be grateful for it.

Unless we are intentional, our life will continue on like the frenzy in those last few seconds before a buzzer signals the game show is over—and we'll miss what's most important in life's second act. Life keeps ticking away, and the number of boxes to check only grows. Get them graduated. Get them out of the house. Get the next promotion. Celebrate the big graduations, birthdays, and anniversaries. Take care of parents. Be present for grandchildren. And while we may long for a pause in our pace, the only pause that comes is hormonal, which can further complicate everything!

Keeping pace in the middle of the race is key to a solid finish. A racer doesn't slow down as they approach the finish. Midlife is our time to celebrate where we're at, contemplate what we've traveled past, and anticipate joyfully what lies ahead. Knowing our purpose in this race propels us to keep moving with both calmness and confidence.

I'd never title myself a runner. I've only finished one official race in my life: the Jingle Bell Run for Arthritis. Christmas music blared through the streets of Washington, DC. Runners wore red and green. Some were dressed as elves or wore Santa caps, and everyone wore bells on their running shoes. It was barely forty degrees outside, but when you're running with hundreds of other people, the chill disappears.

A 5K wasn't like trying to run a marathon. But the energy around me inspired me to run at a much faster pace than usual. When I saw that finish line—though I was exhausted—I didn't slow down. With my goal in sight, I took off in a sprint.

God willing, there's so much life still ahead. We're not winding down—we're figuring out how to enjoy life. What if the attitude we take during these midlife years and beyond sets the tone for however many breaths we're allowed?

Popular culture has conditioned us to think negatively about aging. We're called "over the hill" by age forty. Even the term "middle-aged" is used more often for mockery than applause. The mention of another birthday elicits a comedic groan. It's as if we race to the midway point then question whether or not we're still in good enough shape to keep running.

But instead of listening to the near panic of those who notice their first smile line or invest in every new pricey product to stop signs of aging (if that were even possible), instead of assuming our best years are behind us, what if we use our hard-fought wisdom to change our approach? What if, rather than settle for aging gracefully, we decide to age *gratefully*, looking both behind and ahead with thankful hearts?

> What if, rather than settle for aging gracefully, we decide to age *gratefully*, looking both behind and ahead with thankful hearts?

No, I'll never be the accomplishment-seeking, naive twenty-five-year-old I once was. But I'm grateful for that. What a gift to be alive right here, right now, with more decades worth of wisdom to inform my daily living. Though my physical body notices unwanted changes nearly every day (I give you chin hairs, temperature fluctuations, and gravity's pull), I can look ahead with joyful anticipation when I understand that midlife is a season to flourish. I hope that as you read, you'll be convinced to see midlife with fresh eyes (even if your vision now tops the list of things that have changed).

I don't know about you, but I wasn't comfortable in my own skin even before it sported its first wrinkle. Science tells us our skin starts to age at twenty-five.[1] Our brains start to age at twenty-four.[2] Some say the aging checklist countdown begins when our bodies become adult. We can either focus on those factors or focus on living. It isn't hard to imagine which approach brings more joy and satisfaction.

During the pages that follow, you'll find encouragement and inspiration to discover delight in midlife, later life, or anywhere in between. Aging is more than transitioning to comfortable shoes and monitoring the Weather Channel for rain. We don't slow down as we see more years behind us than ahead of us. We speed up. Not with the kind of frenetic flurry that characterized our twenties. Not like we're contestants on a grocery store game show, desperately accumulating possessions and experiences before time runs out. Instead, we run with purpose.

For some of us, the word *run* is now only metaphorical.

As our trust and faith in Jesus grow, so does our ability to thrive. Because we can look back on His faithfulness and look ahead with hope, we can move forward with greater confidence than ever before. For the next thirty days, let's explore what Scripture says about what it means to embrace aging gratefully.

Day 1

The Secret to Flourishing after Forty

How to Praise as We Age

> They will still bear fruit in old age, they will stay fresh
> and green, proclaiming, "The LORD is upright; he is
> my Rock, and there is no wickedness in him."
> PSALM 92:14–15 (emphasis added)

For more than a decade, I lived outside of Dallas, Texas. The area was all new development—a region that had previously been family farms now boasted residential housing, a Chili's restaurant, and a Walmart. Land that once grew crops and hosted cattle morphed into a proverbial concrete jungle. Mature trees were nowhere to be found.

When we moved into our new home there, the builder planted a tree out front. "Someday," he told us, "it will provide lots of shade for the sunny front window of your daughter's room. But until then, keep the blinds closed."

The first year we had to use props and ropes to keep that little tree upright. Texas is windy in the spring. One giant storm with straight-line winds could knock out billboards and street signs. Our little tree would have to survive adversity before it would ever provide the promised shade.

Year after year my husband cared for that tree. When we moved out of that home, the top of the tree was almost as tall as my daughter's second-floor window. I recently saw a picture of that house online, and guess what? The tree is taller than the roof!

Now we live near Austin, in the heart of Texas Hill Country. Mature trees abound. We have a difficult time maintaining them. They grow quickly and without regular pruning can invade our neighbors' yards. The trees take over the roof, the fence, and anything else in their air space.

These mature trees are one of the reasons we love living here. Today as I look out at the beautiful oak in my front yard, I'm able to visualize and understand some benefits of aging I might have once resisted. Tiny, tethered trees don't have a lot to offer. But mature trees have an unmatched dignity and confidence.

What I see outside my window is impressive: a sturdy trunk, three main branches, each with multiple smaller shoots reaching into the air. Though it's December as I write this, leaves still cover the limbs. Oak trees in Texas don't lose their leaves until the spring. That's right—they flourish right through the winter.

As majestic as this tree is to the eye, I have to imagine that what I don't see is even more impressive. Some of the shallower roots peek through our grass and stretch a full six feet from the trunk. Underneath, there is an even more extensive root system to support this twenty-foot-tall tower and its way to becoming even taller.

The years behind me have allowed me to grow stronger. With solid grounding, I'm free to explore and use my gifts and walk in God's purpose for my life. In my twenties, thirties, and beyond, I floundered internally. Like a sapling, I bent with the wind. I'm grateful God protected me and kept me tethered to Him.

Now, I feel sturdier. I can age gratefully because I know that the more years I've had to mature in Christ, the stronger I am to withstand the storms, stand tall, and flourish for Him.

We've all encountered evidence of trees whose shallow roots made them susceptible to the ravages of drought, pummeling winds, and vandals. How do we invest in the practices that ensure we're deeply rooted for this next season of life's journey?

As always, we take our best cues from Scripture.

God thought the tree metaphor significant enough to choose it throughout Scripture. Psalm 1 tells us the one who delights in the Lord will be like a tree planted by the river. In Psalm 92:12–15 we see the tree in the context of aging:

> The righteous will flourish like a palm tree, they will grow like a cedar of Lebanon; planted in the house of the LORD, they will flourish in the courts of our God. They will still bear fruit in old age, they will stay fresh and green, proclaiming, "The LORD is upright; he is my Rock, and there is no wickedness in him."

What's a biblical tree's secret to aging well? How do they stay fresh and green, youthful, and strong? Earlier in the psalm and then again in verse 15 we find the answer: they praise the Lord.

That can be an important secret of our maturing too—developing deep roots so that we stay connected to our spiritual and emotional "water supply" and turn to praise God, who gave us the privilege of years.

Feeling down about growing older? Praise eases depression (Isaiah 61:3). Feeling restless or anxious, like there's something missing or unaccomplished yet? Praise satisfies our souls (Psalm 63:5). Praise increases our faith and keeps our focus lifted higher—on God and His kingdom instead of the little world we've built around us. It urges our thoughts away from our culture's misunderstanding of the value of aging and toward the only One worthy of a lifelong pursuit.

It's easy to disparage advancing age. I grumble when my knees remind me my running days are long gone. I hesitate to tell my age out loud—not because I'm embarrassed but because it startles me. *Am I really that old?*

What if I turned every opportunity to recognize the fullness of my years into an opportunity to praise God? Could I whisper a prayer of thanks every time I see a picture of the younger me, thanking God for the lessons I've learned since then? What if I could wake up each morning and simply praise Him for a new day? The joy praise brings may snuff out those "I feel old" sighs.

Look at what Paul says about our need to praise in Hebrews 13:15–16: "Through Jesus, therefore, let us *continually* offer to God a sacrifice of praise—the fruit of lips that openly profess his name. And do not forget to do good and to share with others, for with such sacrifices God is pleased" (emphasis added). May we continually offer our praise to God and view our maturity of years as the blessing God intended it to be.

Today I can be grateful that the roots of my faith, the trunk of my confidence, and the branches of my courage have grown to help me flourish.

Prayer

Dear Heavenly Father, please help my heart to be grateful for the privilege of aging and the opportunity I have to continue to grow in and through you. Remind

me often of the sturdy tree and the foundational work
you've done. Teach me to praise you continually.

Aging Gratefully in Action

Commit to intentional praise each day. Stay rooted in praise as your whole self stays rooted in God. Choose a favorite worship song to sing, or declare your thanksgiving and admiration for God out loud while you drive, or whisper your praise to Him while you work. He is worthy of our praise, and praising Him as we age is key to flourishing.

Wisdom of Years

Age Is Not a Disadvantage

So teach us to number our days that we
may get a heart of wisdom.
PSALM 90:12 ESV

Isn't it ironic how we spend a significant portion of our youth anticipating our next birthday, only to reach some elusive number and wish for youth again?

As children, we corrected adults who dismissively captured age in whole numbers. "Excuse me—I'm nine and a half!" The teen years come, and we count the minutes until we can get behind the wheel or cast a vote. Sixteen, eighteen, twenty-one—they're not just milestones, they're rites of passage. For a while, happiness swells with more candles on your cake.

Only the young round up.

One day we stop counting years and start adding decades. Soon we have to check the county's fire risk report before we dare make the number of candles accurate on that birthday cake. When someone asks our age, we don't intentionally mislead. We forget how old we are because—at some point—we stopped keeping track.

I've often wondered why Scripture instructs us to count our days. It's hard enough to tally the years. In Psalm 90:12 we read, "Teach us to number our days that we may get a heart of wisdom" (ESV). A heart of wisdom sounds great, but is there an app for that counting part? Math is harder than it used to be.

When I think of counting days, I picture a prisoner marking slashes on his cell wall to track the passing time. This can't be what the psalmist meant. Surely the intended tone isn't one of doom and dread or one more day (or year) stuck in the cell. We're not checking off dates like finished items on a to-do list.

The origins of Psalm 90 are unique. The chapter is titled "A prayer of Moses the man of God." It's the only song of Moses found in the Psalms. The lyrics recount the greatness of God. Moses remembers how powerful God has shown himself to be and how He had led His people out of slavery and toward the promised land.

Then Moses juxtaposes how God counts time versus how we do. Poetically he compares God's infinite greatness with a human's short life span. In Psalm 90:9–10 he writes, "For all our days pass away under your wrath; we bring our years to an end like a sigh. The years of our life are seventy, or even by reason of strength eighty; yet their span is but toil and trouble; they are soon gone, and we fly away" (ESV). (All the octogenarians I know would probably remind me that, regarding life span, this was written in a different era. And not for Americans. Moses rounded down.)

Moses had wandered around the wilderness for decades, and in fact, he was 80 before he began his trek, and he died at 120! He toiled. He labored. He suffered. And yet he sees the insignificance of anything we do on earth, any years we exist, when compared to God and His bigger picture of time and space.

But if the message is that God is big and endless and I am not, how does tracking my life in even smaller increments help? Perhaps He wants us to remember that our journey through this life is precious. Unless we make extra effort to count, consider, and pay attention, we'll miss the moments as we number the years.

I grew up in Pennsylvania. Every summer we took at least one trip south to Florida. By the time we hit Virginia, I knew exactly how far it was to the South Carolina line because of the advertising efforts of a rest-stop-meets-tourist-trap called "South of the Border." It was tacky and culturally insensitive. But their billboards were hard to miss and even harder to forget. You'd see signs for their snack bar and gift shop at least a hundred miles before you'd see their signature giant sombrero.

As a child I diligently watched for these signs along the highway. Each featured the official spokesman, Pedro, touting the virtues of making a stop. Thirty miles to clean restrooms! Ten miles to ten-dollar T-shirts! Pedro says, "You need candy!" Each amplified my anticipation. Isn't this what most of us do on road trips? We focus on the milestones and not the mile markers.

Now that I'm older, I see how I have the same tendencies when traveling through life. I focus on calendar days that are full, not empty. I too often live from event to event, missing what's in between. I'm tempted to focus on the next holiday weekend, vacation, or celebration and miss the everyday opportunities God grants me. What would it look like to treat weeknight dinners, trips to the grocery store, or walks to the mailbox like God-ordained moments?

Maybe this is why Moses encourages us to enumerate the

ordinary. When we count only the milestones, we miss those mile markers—the minutes, the hours, and the days that characterize our lives. Granted, it may have driven my parents mad if I'd read every little green sign along the highway. Yet how much do I miss because I'm dreaming about what's fifty miles ahead?

> **When we count only the milestones, we miss those mile markers—the minutes, the hours, and the days that characterize our lives.**

The apostle Paul reiterates Moses's message in Ephesians 5:15–16 when he says, "So be careful how you live. Don't live like fools, but like those who are wise. Make the most of every opportunity in these evil days" (NLT). It's easy to get so caught up in life that we miss out on living it for God and His kingdom. We steward our time well when we see it as a gift God's granted us to use for Him.

Today I can be grateful for the freedom to live each day—both the ordinary and the extraordinary—to the fullest for God's glory. I can be thankful for each milestone and mile marker I've passed, knowing they are gifts from God. I can find rest in the knowledge that He holds each day, each month, and each year securely in His hands.

Prayer

Dear Heavenly Father, help me see you in the day-to-day, minute-to-minute life I lead. Father, show me how to make the most of each day for your kingdom and glory. Help me not to overlook the ordinary but to look for your beauty in it.

Aging Gratefully in Action

Being fully present is difficult in our era. It's easy to get caught up in other worlds through our entertainment and our media. But being in the moment, especially when we're with others, is a beautiful gift. Younger generations chronically struggle to put down their screens and engage, but we are not immune. If you find yourself spending a lot of time staring at electronic devices, consider these suggestions. Try implementing a no-phones-at-the-table rule for meals, take a screen sabbath on a Saturday afternoon, or, if you're married, talk to your spouse about creating a screen-free hour to connect before bed. The nonstop availability of distractions can keep us from fully experiencing some of the most meaningful moments of our lives.

Seeing God's Statistics

Embracing the Opportunity to See God's Faithfulness

He who began a good work in you will
carry it on to completion.
PHILIPPIANS 1:6

When you claim Texas as home, you either like football or get left out of conversations. Fortunately I've been a Dallas Cowboys fan for decades. So when my husband decided to attend seminary in the Big D (Dallas), I knew there'd be more football in my future.

While I enjoy watching and cheering for my team, there's one part of televised sports I don't understand or appreciate: the statistics. He has this run average. This team is "two and nine" for away games. The kicker makes 60 percent of all kicks from this yard line. Does anyone really care about all this data? I don't. *Yawn.*

But I may have misjudged their benefits. The stats can show how the team has improved or where they need development.

Stats reveal victories that may have been years or decades in the making. Even the losses tally shows the challenge that lies ahead and what it will take to overcome.

Looking at the stats in our lives may have similar benefits. In fact, one of the things I treasure most about aging is the ability to trace back through the years of my life and look at God's record of faithfulness. It's not just the blessing of seeing how he protected and sustained me through my teens or twenties. Now decades of trials and triumphs, long valleys I've endured, and proverbial peaks I've summited contribute to the stats. I have a litany of experiences to reflect on whenever I find myself wondering, *Will God really show up again?*

I'm reminded of one of these stories every time I brush my teeth. My gums started aging long before the rest of me. At age thirty-three, the periodontist told me I had the mouth of someone decades older. How was my mouth aging faster than the rest of my body?

The pink flesh surrounding my teeth started pulling away in rebellion. The gum-grafting surgery was expensive. It had only been a few weeks since I'd delivered my second baby, and my husband, Eric, was leaving his military career to head to seminary. Though we'd been saving, money would be tight as we stepped away from careers and entered full-time ministry. Ten thousand dollars to save my teeth was not in the budget.

Eric accompanied me on the final consult before my surgery. The periodontist practically swooned over fighter pilots, so they hit it off immediately. But, when Eric told him he was leaving his California *Top Gun* life to serve Jesus, the gum doc looked disappointed. He responded with, "I can't believe anyone would leave a great career to do something for a silly religion."

He thought we were crazy.

Surgery day came and went. The only issue outstanding was the bill. Insurance would help a bit. We needed to see what was left.

Every night my husband prayed God would take care of that bill. And secretly, every night, I thought, *Brace yourself, dear man. We're going to be writing a big check. There's no other way. That doctor isn't even a Christian.*

Months passed, and Eric kept praying. We settled into our new lives in Dallas, and one day, finally, the envelope arrived. I opened it and could not believe what I saw. The balance—which equaled thousands of dollars—was crossed off. On the invoice was a stamp that said "Paid in full!" along with a personal note from the periodontist that said, "Good luck in Texas." I still cry when I think about how God provided for my failing gums.

That's one story. One statistic revealing God's creative ways of providing for our needs. In your history there also lies a collection of stories of His faithfulness.

In Psalm 103:2, we're encouraged to "Praise the LORD . . . and forget not all his benefits." In Deuteronomy 8, God instructs His people, through Moses, to make remembering a practice. In verse 2, we read, "And you shall remember the whole way that the LORD your God has led you these forty years in the wilderness, that he might humble you, testing you to know what was in your heart, whether you would keep his commandments or not" (ESV).

No matter what the wilderness of our life looks like, God is still there. His goodness to us is proven by the way He's been faithful not just in our stories but throughout history. Psalm 100:5 encourages us with these words: "For the LORD is good; his steadfast love endures forever, and his faithfulness to all generations" (ESV). Praise God for that.

Today I can be grateful that God's statistics are always impressive. Now that I'm older, I have a collection of stories that allow me to see God's faithfulness at play in my life. Though I should know that God always bats a thousand (or whatever sports statistic analogy you prefer), I'm grateful that now, in midlife, I can remember His excellent track record. When I doubt that God sees, hears, or cares, I can remember and be reminded of just how much He has seen, heard, and cared—and still does!

Prayer

---

*Dear Heavenly Father, help me to remember your statistics
in my life. When I'm tempted to fear or doubt, remind me
of the times you've been faithful. Show me how you've never
failed me. Help me embrace the years that lie ahead with
a record book full of your goodness and kindness to me.*

Aging Gratefully in Action

A joyful heart is better than medicine, Scripture tells us. It's also better than expensive antiaging formulas, wrinkle concealers, spa treatment, and beauty supplements. When you think about God's statistics in your life, write them down to count the ways God has been good to you. See what kind of joy emanates from you when you meditate on the ways God has been faithful.

Thriving in a New Season

Thanking God for the Next Season of Life

For everything there is a season, and a time
for every matter under heaven.
ECCLESIASTES 3:1 ESV

Growing up on the East Coast, we had four distinct seasons, and back-to-school time meant carrying a jacket. But in Texas seasons are confusing. By October I'm weary of the summer clothes I've worn since April. I envy women on television who sit in New York studios wearing cozy sweaters and boots. I'd be a puddle of melted Mary Kay if I tried to double layer my knees or elbows in early autumn. The real trick-or-treat at the end of October is guessing whether or not the temperature will exceed ninety.

Yet even in central Texas, summer eventually concedes defeat. November comes. The leaves are so shocked, they turn orange overnight. There's no gradual lead-up. It's just *surprise! Welcome to fall!*

Sometimes the seasons in our life change gradually. But other times seasons shift Texas-style. One day your life is bottles and blankies, and the next you're sending out graduation announcements. Maybe you felt comfortable in your town, job, or marriage, when suddenly the season changed without warning. Midlife can be filled with jolts and shifts.

There's a woman in the Bible who endured a series of extreme season changes. Famine drove her away from everything she knew, out of Bethlehem into the land of Moab. No doubt the journey was traumatic for Naomi, but at least she had her husband and boys by her side.

Then tragedy struck. First, Naomi lost her husband. Then her boys died too. Naomi felt like her life was over. How many winters could she endure? She tried to send her daughters-in-law away so they could have a chance at better days. But one of these women refused to leave Naomi's side. Her name was Ruth.

Perhaps you know what happens next, but how often do we consider this story from Naomi's perspective? She went from full house to empty nest in an instant. As a widow with no remaining sons, she stood stripped of her standing, resources, and hope. Talk about an unexpected change of seasons! It was as if the first day of winter hit with a full-on blizzard.

When I read this story as a youth, I thought Naomi was being dramatic when she told her family to call her Mara, which means *bitter*. But now that I'm older, I sympathize with her plight. I'm sure Naomi doubted that spring would ever come. I would've too.

But Naomi's story doesn't end there. God had a rescue plan. When Ruth reported to Naomi how a man named Boaz was offering kindness to her, I picture the twinkle returning to Naomi's tired eyes. Eventually Boaz became the one who restored both Ruth and Naomi to a place of security and status. Ruth and Boaz had a son named Obed. Scripture says he was named by the women of the neighborhood as they marveled at the fact that Naomi had a son again!

In Ruth 4:15, we read that the women said to Naomi, "He will renew your life and sustain you in your old age. For your daughter-in-law, who loves you and who is better to you than seven sons, has given him birth." Naomi's story wasn't over yet.

We long for fruitful lives. It sounds appealing to live in spring-time forever. But that's not how seasons work. I don't know why God created this pattern in nature or in our lives, but it's clear He did. There are short summers, wearisome winters, invigorating springs, and arduous autumns. Midlife season changes include watching children grow into adults while parents grow into dependents. Our job titles may shift as we age out of or into roles at work. From menopausal mood swings to delayed dreams to difficult diagnoses, seasons seem to come and go more rapidly as I age.

How can we learn to embrace new seasons? There are two concepts I find helpful. We must both believe and grieve. Yes, we have to trust the only One who doesn't change. We can have complete confidence that God is not surprised by what's happening in our lives. As the psalmist says in Psalm 31:15, "My times are in your hands." John 10:28 reminds us that no one can snatch us out of God's hand, while Ecclesiastes clearly shows us that seasons are a part of life. We can believe that God holds the future.

We know that even as our roles, relationships, and realities change, the One who controls them all does not. When we lose our sense of direction trying to navigate the new world of the next season, we can believe that God created the map and knows where He's taking us.

In addition to believing that God has a good plan for what's ahead, sometimes entering a new season also requires us to grieve. We think of grief when we lose someone close to us. But grief aptly applies to the seasonal changes that accompany aging. We may grieve that we're no longer needed to pack lunches or help with homework. We may grieve that the decades have flown by much faster than we expected. Or we may grieve that life doesn't look or feel like we expected it would. Facing the loss of faded dreams or shattered expectations can require as much grieving as a death in the family.

Grief can look like anger, denial, bargaining, or depression before we accept the loss. The process isn't neat and linear. Grief never RSVPs to let you know it's coming. Instead the sadness may take over your body every time you walk past that empty bedroom, hear that song, or watch a new baby get dedicated at church. None of us can avoid grief, but viewing grief as a healthy part of aging and an important part of the process of healing can help us move forward and leave much of the pain behind.

Moving freely into a new season requires that we be present enough to process the change. To do that, we believe God has a good plan for what's ahead while acknowledging the beauty of what is no longer. Knowing that we are never alone on our journey can bring us comfort in the here and now, even when our hearts long most for the comforts of the past.

Today I can be grateful that the God who organized creation into seasons knew exactly what He was doing when He built seasons into my life too. The same God who was with Naomi through her seasons of change can restore hope and new life to my soul through Jesus. I don't have to feel afraid when it's time to pull out the boots and sweaters for life's wintery blast. God goes with me.

Prayer

Dear Heavenly Father, thank you for the gift of new seasons. Thank you for the reprieve at the end of hard seasons and for your sustaining grace as we journey into winters we never anticipated. Your Word says you will never leave us or forsake us. Help me to remember that you are always with me as the seasons of my life change.

Aging Gratefully in Action

Are you embracing a new season, or are you still wearing your summer clothes in December? Part of the grieving process of aging may be to clean out your closet. What items of clothing are you keeping just because you're not quite ready to accept that season as finished? Are there clothes that no longer fit or that you no longer need in your current roles that still hang in your closet? If so, pause and pray about how the physical act of cleaning out your closet may help you more fully accept the new season you're in.

Unwavering Confidence

Trusting the One Who Never Fails

Have I not commanded you? Be strong and courageous.
Do not be afraid; do not be discouraged, for the Lord
your God will be with you wherever you go.
JOSHUA 1:9

I'm mostly an extrovert. Speaking on stage in front of large groups doesn't bother me. But put me in a small circle and commission everyone to say their name, where they're from, and something clever about themselves, and I'll experience physical symptoms of anxiety. My palms will sweat. Other parts will do the same. I'll rehearse my answer in my head a few hundred times. As my turn approaches, nausea in my stomach will work its way up my esophagus.

That wave of nervousness that comes when entering a room of new people didn't disappear at midlife. As a child or teen, I would've guessed that middle-aged women always feel confident. After all, waiting around for Mom to stop talking was a regular pastime. Teachers, coaches, and other adult women I observed never seemed to struggle to make friends or carry on conversations. I looked forward to the day when I'd feel that way too.

But I still haven't reached the age where confidence comes baked into the birthday cake. It's ironic that we expect to be confident when we're older. Then we reach a particular age and lose our confidence because we're no longer as young as we used to be. It's a confidence conundrum.

Scripture talks a lot about confidence. But while we tend to stress over how to be braver, bolder, or more beautiful, self-confidence isn't the Bible's theme. In fact, even the primary definition of the word *confidence* in the *Merriam-Webster* dictionary has little to do with feeling fabulous. Rock-solid confidence comes from rock-solid beliefs.

While culture shouts to focus on my own strength and goodness, I know that's not God's answer. No matter how much I try to believe I can do it on my own, there's no security there. I fail too often. Chasing self-confidence is like running on a treadmill. You can invest the time and sweat, but you'll never actually get anywhere.

Fortunately, the gospel offers a different path to confidence. Because of Jesus, I'm strongest when I am weak. God is the only place I can put my confidence where it will never be shaken. Though self-confidence sounds like a nice goal, more God confidence is what I need to navigate the uncertainty of aging. While I'm changing in more ways than I can count, God remains unchangeable. I can feel secure in Him, even when I'm insecure about what's going on around or inside of me.

Look at these instructions in Jeremiah 9:23–24:

> Thus says the LORD: "Let not the wise man boast
> in his wisdom, let not the mighty man boast in

his might, let not the rich man boast in his riches, but let him who boasts boast in this, that he understands and knows me, that I am the LORD who practices steadfast love, justice, and righteousness in the earth. For in these things I delight, declares the LORD." (ESV)

The apostle Paul also reminds us that God confidence is far more desirable than self-confidence. In 2 Corinthians 10:17–18, Paul references the Jeremiah passage and explains, "But, 'Let the one who boasts boast in the Lord.' For it is not the one who commends himself who is approved, but the one whom the Lord commends."

Then again, in Hebrews 10:35–36, we're reminded, "So do not throw away this confident trust in the Lord. Remember the great reward it brings you! Patient endurance is what you need now, so that you will continue to do God's will. Then you will receive all that he has promised" (NLT). When Paul talks of confidence, he encourages believers to know the One in whom they can safely put their trust.

When Joshua took over for Moses, he had big sandals to fill. It was up to him to take this next generation of Israelites into the promised land. For their whole lives, they'd heard of this place. I can only imagine how high their expectations must have been and the pressure Joshua must have felt.

And yet Joshua seemed confident. Not because he exercised regularly and knew he had the battle smarts. I don't picture Joshua flexing in front of the mirror, chanting, "I got this." His confidence came from the firm belief that he could rely completely on God. He had rock-solid trust in the One who had rescued them from slavery and led them, faithfully, through the desert.

The secret to feeling confident has nothing to do with age, appearance, or accomplishment. Instead it's about getting better at the practice of placing my confidence where it belongs. Though it's tempting to believe I'm now old enough or experienced enough to handle whatever life throws my way, maturity means leaning on the rock more, not less. Maturity means understanding that I have no ability to go it on my own. Without the stability of that rock, I will fall.

So how does this help when I sit in that circle of strangers and it's my turn to share? I can have confidence that, because of Jesus, I don't have to put hope in winning the admiration of others. No matter how nervous my body feels, I can rest securely in the truth that it's His opinion of me that matters most. As I practice turning my focus to the true source of my confidence, I've found my physical body learns to relax too. It follows the lead of what I believe.

Today I can be grateful that as I age, my confidence in my unchanging God can grow. I don't have to fear the future because I know my God is trustworthy. The One who created the universe and holds the stars in His hands has everything under His control. Though my palms may sweat or my hands may tremble, when I put my trust in Him, I can never be shaken.

Prayer

Dear Heavenly Father, show me what it means to derive my confidence from you. Show me how to live a life that isn't marked by fear but by trust in your faithfulness. Grow my faith so that I am firmly rooted in Christ. Help me not to rely on my own ability to muster up courage. Rather, remind me to tap into the courage God promises when I place my confidence in Him alone.

Aging Gratefully in Action

Nothing makes a person more attractive than a smile. Studies show this to be true. Smiling activates tiny molecules in your brain that help you fight stress. So when you feel fear creeping in or anxiety overwhelming you, curl your lips upward and smile. It's more soothing than you realize. A smile that comes from a woman who derives her confidence from Christ alone is a beautiful sight.

Over Obsession

The Joy of Being Free from the Ideal Me

Whoever dwells in the shelter of the Most High will rest in
the shadow of the Almighty. I will say of the LORD, "He is
my refuge and my fortress, my God, in whom I trust."
PSALM 91:1–2

It's easy to have a perfect life. As long as you never leave the
confines of your imagination, that is. I know this scheme
well. I plotted exactly what kind of life I would have. I'd
rise early in the morning to wake my children to the scent of
freshly scrambled eggs and oven-crisped bacon. My joy would
be as full as my coffee cup after I'd spent an hour in devotions
and another hour exercising my body. I'd sing my way through
household chores like a cartoon princess. My children would
always reply in obedience, our home would be spotless, and my
husband would be so enamored with me that he'd never even
turn on the television.

Of course, that ideal me lived only in my head. She couldn't seem to show up on time for any other occasion. Real life has looked drastically different than my imagined version. Now, as I've cruised past the midlife point, I have two options. I can accept the distinction between my ideals and my reality, or I can continue to carry the pressure and shame that come from not being able to compete with the fantasy version of myself.

I choose door number one.

In my book *The Burden of Better*, I talk about how tricky it is to navigate the problem of comparison when the person we're comparing ourselves to lives mostly in our minds. I've met many women over the years who aren't caught up in trying to look or be more like that woman on a billboard or the neighbor down the street. Instead they're stuck trying to be more like the person they once daydreamed they would be. They feel guilt and condemnation for their own inability to become their idealized selves.

But why? How is it that we can feel so bad about not achieving a set of standards or goals that we secretly hold? Why do my ideals have so much power? It's because ideals become idols.

Dreams that are held too tightly become entangled in our identity. When goals and fantasies become more important to me than the purpose-filled life in Christ that God has planned, I create idols. I believe that these dreams for my life will satisfy me.

Yet when I strive for my ideals, I make life harder than God ever intended. He never asked me to write a separate list of what I need in order to have satisfaction and joy. He already completed the list and completed the work. His answer is straightforward: Jesus is what you need.

Though I believe this to be true, my answer has often been, "Yes, I need Jesus and a self-improvement plan!" Or "I hear you, Jesus . . . I know you've got the big stuff taken care of, but my life will be better once I shape up my body, remodel the house, and get everything else just the way I want it."

Oh how the pursuit of my goals has led me to some desperate places! The older I get, the more grateful I am that some of my dreams didn't come true. Culture's definition of success had too great an influence on my vision board. There are many areas in which I can be thankful that my life hasn't turned out like I hoped it would.

Jesus didn't match anyone's definition of an ideal savior. The Jews were searching for a political leader who would rescue them from Rome's oppression. I doubt I would have seen it either. I get so focused, looking for things to match my definition of the way they should be, that I likely would have had the same reaction.

Have you ever heard of your mind's eye? We use the expression to describe our ability to visualize or imagine something that's already happened or that we'd like to happen. It's that part of our brains that allows us to watch bits of our lives as vividly as we watch a Netflix movie. As I read Romans 12:1–2, which instructs us to be transformed by the renewing of our minds, I wonder if Jesus also wants to transform what I imagine—if He wants to take my dreams and give them a makeover too.

Midlife offers a unique opportunity to stop and take inventory of where life's ideals may never match reality. A coaching client recently confessed that she and her best friend realized they'd been chasing the same earthly dreams for forty years. At her fiftieth birthday party, they made a pact to stop the insanity of doing the same things and hoping for different results. They recognized that it was time to refresh their goals and align them more with God's.

Isaiah 55:8–9 reminds us, "'My thoughts are nothing like your thoughts,' says the Lord. 'And my ways are far beyond anything you could imagine. For just as the heavens are higher than the earth, so my ways are higher than your ways and my thoughts higher than your thoughts'" (NLT). My plans for a more ideal life will always fall short of what God has planned for me.

C. S. Lewis uses a wonderful illustration about how our greatest dreams for our lives pale compared to God's. He writes, "We are half-hearted creatures, fooling about with drink and sex and ambition when infinite joy is offered us, like an ignorant child who wants to go on making mud pies in a slum because he cannot imagine what is meant by the offer of a holiday at the sea. We are far too easily pleased."[3]

Likewise, God's definition of joy is far superior to my definition of personal happiness. This earth was never intended to satisfy me. Every pursuit apart from Jesus will disappoint. We hope that happiness, peace, joy, and rest will be found at the end of our strivings, but idols never deliver on their promises.

Today I can be grateful that through Jesus, my strivings can cease. I'm not giving up on my ideals because I've become a jaded pragmatist. Instead, I can surrender my ideals because I see how easily they turn into idols that attempt to lead me away from Jesus. He's the only true model for a perfect life.

Prayer

Thank you, Heavenly Father, that you have freed me to be who you created me to be. Continue to release me from these standards and expectations I put on myself that are outside of what you've asked of me. Help me to see the reality of how my ideals become my idols.

Aging Gratefully in Action

Write a list of the expectations that you have for yourself at this stage of life. Now, compare these expectations to what you know about the truth of Scripture. Are these expectations that

God has for you and your life, or are these extras? When we are free to serve and love God without being encumbered by the self-imposed pressures and expectations—that's when we're free to let His beauty shine.

The Greatest Beauty

*Recognizing the Most Beautiful Thing
about Us Is Inside, Not Out*

Rather, it should be that of your inner self, the
unfading beauty of a gentle and quiet spirit,
which is of great worth in God's sight.

1 PETER 3:4

Some days the mirror is unkind. My reflection seems to
capture my attention most when I'm feeling discouraged.
Plans fell through. The yes I expected turned out to be
a no. A relationship feels strained. Or all these things at once!
Then I look in the mirror.

And by "look" in the mirror, I mean I take a long, hard stare
into that glass. I hope, in vain, that I'll find a reason to be encouraged there. Of course, that never works. It never has. If
my reflection wasn't good enough for me at nine, nineteen, or
twenty-nine . . . how silly of me to think I could find the affirmation I crave there today.

Why do I turn more focus to the mirror in times of stress or disappointment? What am I really searching for? I think it's beauty. Like a singular flower growing in the middle of the weeds, I long to see a glimmer of life springing out of the dirt. We're wired to desire beauty.

But the beauty I seek will never be found on the outside of this aging body. I love God's care in emphasizing this truth to us in several places in Scripture. He knew we'd be tempted to find satisfaction in the superficial. So He kindly and gently reminds us that external beauty is never as valuable as we believe. In 1 Samuel 16:7, God reminds Samuel that He doesn't look at our outward appearance but at our hearts. Likewise, Jeremiah 17:10 reemphasizes that God tests us according to our hearts and our deeds. The psalmist reiterates the importance of having a clean, pure heart.

True beauty isn't about being five foot nine and model thin, with flowing hair and flawless skin. Beauty is more than a magazine picture. True beauty is a life lived in surrender to Jesus.

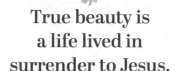

True beauty is a life lived in surrender to Jesus.

Peter has instructions for the women of the early church. He tells them that their true beauty isn't in their ability to wear fancy clothes or look attractive. In 1 Peter 3:4, he teaches that beauty "should be that of your inner self, the unfading beauty of a gentle and quiet spirit, which is of great worth in God's sight."

This kind of true beauty happens through the sanctification of our hearts as they're transformed in submission to the Savior. It's only through this submission that I can have this gentle and quiet spirit Peter mentions. When my pursuit of beauty is external, my heart is disrupted and unsettled. It's never enough. True beauty in midlife looks like peace. True beauty in midlife looks like treating others—and ourselves—gently.

Launching children, caring for elderly parents, coping with fluctuating hormones, and everything else that midlife offers can feel anything but peaceful. Life is constantly changing. There's no security if we look around us to find stability and safety. It can only be found in the arms of God.

Truth is, security and safety are the reasons we're tempted to chase culture's definition of beauty instead of God's. We believe the lie that if we could just look good enough, then we'd feel that peace we long for. We'd be safe from the criticism of ourselves and others. We'd be secure and confident if we wore the "right" size or could fool people into thinking we're ten years younger. Secretly we may wrestle the same desire to fit in as we did in middle school.

But true beauty isn't desperate for a seat at the cool kids' lunch spot. It rests securely at Jesus's table. In fact, even better than just sharing a meal with Him, we know that in Him we have unrivaled belonging.

Psalm 23 may be the most recited passage of the entire Old Testament. We're given many pictures throughout the passage of who God is in relationship to us. He is the shepherd; we are His sheep. He is our guide as we climb mountains of difficulties and as we rest in green pastures. Yet He also sits with us at the table He has prepared. He fills our cups so much that they overflow!

These six verses communicate security and safety to our insecure hearts. When we feel rattled by midlife, Jesus holds us. He is my shepherd. I shall not want because I don't need anything else. I am secure in Him.

Though our outer beauty may feel like it's fading (at least by *Vogue*'s definition), maybe that's necessary to letting our true beauty shine through. With gentle and quiet spirits, we can feel at peace in our aging bodies and secure in our acceptance through Christ.

Today I can be grateful that my greatest beauty can radiate from my heart. It may never be captured in photos or my reflection in the glass, yet this kind of true beauty isn't dampened by aging or stifled by hard seasons. Instead, it has even more opportunities to flourish as I continue to submit to my Savior.

Prayer

Dear Heavenly Father, help me today to learn to worship true beauty—your beauty—instead of the beauty this world has taught me to praise. Help me to cultivate the gentle and quiet spirit that comes from submitting to you and resting in your grace.

Aging Gratefully in Action

If you find the mirror to be a stumbling block—a place where you find yourself discouraged or disheartened—consider taking a break from it. I call this a "mirror fast." Of course, that doesn't mean you never look in the mirror. But for thirty days, try to use the mirror only when necessary—like applying makeup or fixing your hair. Avoid staring into it for too long, and avoid other opportunities to examine how you look on the outside. You may be amazed at how free you feel when you spend less time focused on how you look.

Zippers, Snaps, and Other Annoyances

Understanding Body Image as You Age

The glory of young men is their strength, but
the splendor of old men is their gray hair.
PROVERBS 20:29 ESV

Even a great day can be spoiled by a zipper that won't zip, a snap that won't stay shut, or a button and hole that can no longer comfortably make the trip to connect like they once did. Is it just me, or do our clothes get less cooperative as we age? One day the pants fit just fine. Then you pull them out of your closet a season or two later and wonder how you ever previously got them on.

Giving fastening tools the ability to spoil our day seems silly. And yet who among us feels good when clothes that once fit well are now a little too tight? Our minds react to this occurrence with fear and dread. *Oh no. My body is changing. What am I going to do about it?* Or worse: *Can I do anything about it?*

But here's a reality we prefer not to acknowledge: bodies change. Our bodies change day by day, week by week, and year by year. We're not made of plastic, so there's no other option. From the moment we're born, we never stop changing. That's natural, the way God made us. And yet we feel shame around it.

In the 2015 movie *The Age of Adaline*, a woman survives a mysterious accident that somehow renders her unable to age physically. Perhaps you're thinking, *Wow, what a great problem to have!* But, as the plotline reveals, the inability to look old isn't the blessing one might expect.

Adaline's physical appearance remains that of a twenty-five-year-old woman, yet her mind and the world around her continue to grow and change. As she nears eighty, her daughter looks like her grandmother. She fends off advances from men who are sixty years her junior. She struggles in relationships because, as she explains in the movie, "What good is love if there's no growing old together?"

In many ways this plotline offers a jolt to those of us who've pined to look like we did in our twenties or thirties. Invisible aging lacks authenticity. God created us as whole beings, minds, spirits, and bodies. For the aging process to be segmented to just one aspect of ourselves would feel more like frustration than freedom.

Body image as we age means letting go of expectations we once held for our bodies. This isn't easy. We wonder why our bodies can't do what they used to do effortlessly. Then we remember our age. We feel a flash of understanding that is too often followed by a mini wave of guilt. What should I be doing to fix that?

But what if the biggest gift of aging is recognizing that our bodies are not improvement projects? What if our bodies were created, just as they are, on purpose and for a purpose? There's no follow-up verse to Ephesians 2:10 (NLT) that says we're God's masterpieces but only until age forty! What if God is not surprised that these bodies He gave us look different now than they did at sixteen or twenty-six?

While we fight our changing bodies, lengthening the "needs fixed" list with each passing year, I wonder if God isn't waiting for us to surrender.

Of course, surrender doesn't look like giving up on caring for ourselves. Instead, surrender means saying, "God, can you use me? Show me your kingdom purpose for which I was made. Turn my focus toward using my body for your glory! Free me from the need to try to perfect my body to receive glory of its own."

The New Testament story of two sisters, Mary and Martha, has been used countless times to illustrate the difference between longing to be and longing to do. Of course, Scripture doesn't tell us whether Martha was always on a diet and Mary ate whatever she wanted—but the lesson as to what each valued while in the presence of Jesus offers insight into our battles with body image as we age.

Martha, she's the fixer. Having known some fixers over the years, I can imagine she paid keen attention to how her tunic fit and noticed when it hugged a little tighter. She's got a plan though. She wants to get everything just right. I relate so much to Martha. And I don't believe God is shaming her for being a doer. Martha's sin isn't in the doing. It's in what she's prioritizing.

Jesus wants us to have our priorities in order. To put the doing behind the being. To let His presence guide our doing in every day and every interaction. Let's look at Martha's interaction with Jesus in Luke 10:40–42.

But Martha was distracted with much serving. And she went up to him and said, "Lord, do you not care that my sister has left me to serve alone? Tell her then to help me." But the Lord answered her, "Martha, Martha, you are anxious and troubled about many things, but one thing is necessary. Mary has chosen the good portion, which will not be taken away from her." (ESV)

Anxious and troubled about many things? Oh my! I know Jesus would say the same to me. I hear Him asking why I feel troubled that the jeans I wore at age thirty no longer fit. I know He'd tell me the same: "Choose what is necessary. Focus on what won't be taken away. Wearing a certain size is what's most important in your kingdom, not in mine."

Regardless of my tactics to keep my body young, aging is inevitable. The years will take their toll on this dust-formed body. Sure, I can make wise choices for my health. But what's most important is not preserving my body as if it were going on display in a museum. What's of most value is spending the time I have left in this body worshiping Jesus and telling others about Him.

> **When I recognize that my purpose here is not to please the mirror but my Savior, I'm free to reflect the One in whose image I am made.**

The best news is that knowing God and making Him known doesn't require us to look twenty-five. When I recognize that my purpose here is not to please the mirror but my Savior, I'm free to reflect the One in whose image I am made. I can tilt my mirror up and be free to reflect His beauty.

When we lament losing the bodies of our youth, what we really fear is being forgotten and overlooked, unseen, or unloved. But God promises to never leave us or forsake us. Like God demonstrated to Hagar in Genesis 16:13, He is El Roi, the God who sees. There's no age limit on that.

Today I can be grateful that God will always notice me. Even when I feel like I'm aging out of life's imaginary beauty contest, God isn't surprised by my aging body. In fact, He sees it as beautiful and good. As Proverbs 20:29 reminds, "The glory of the young is their strength; the gray hair of experience is the splendor of the old" (NLT).

The truth is, it would be strange not to age. Like in *Age of Adaline*, perhaps our wish to never look old would be more of a curse than a blessing. What if there's no shame in allowing aging to take its course, even if that means suffering through the annoyance of wardrobe malfunctions?

Prayer

Dear Heavenly Father, help me surrender to the truth that you made my body good and aging is okay. Please help me recognize when I'm wrestling with defining beauty in the way the world defines it instead of the way your Word defines it. Teach me how to see my body the way you do.

Aging Gratefully in Action

You've cleaned out your closet—now it's time to tackle those drawers. What items of clothing have been lingering in there for years, untouched? It may be time to let go of the shame and gently accept that items that fit perfectly a few years ago may not be right for your body now. If your body is allowed to age authentically, then your clothing sizes and styles will need to adapt with it. Take each item you remove and thank God for any joyful memories connected to it. Then donate that top, those shorts, or the jeans to a women's shelter. What takes up space in your drawers could bring great blessing to others.

Gaining Wait

Making Peace with Your Body

Even to your old age and gray hairs, I am he, I am
he who will sustain you. I have made you and I will
carry you; I will sustain you and I will rescue you.
ISAIAH 46:4

ose Ten Pounds in Ten Days!"
Now that's an article I'd read! Twice. Some people are
tempted by get-rich-quick schemes or fame. I'm tempted
by crash diets, pills, and programs that promise to quickly solve
my battle of the bulge.

You see, shortly after my fortieth birthday, I was diagnosed
with an autoimmune thyroid issue. My doctor suspected that
my adrenal glands were also wearing out. Overexercising and
constantly requiring my body to run without enough calories
triggered my body to stay in a constant state of stress. All my
years of dieting had taken their toll, and I was sentenced to

life with the consequences. Losing weight would now be harder than ever.

But instead of hearing "slow down, trust God, and take better care of your body," I continued on my quest to find the magic cure. I bought the books, read the blog posts, and procured the plans to help me overcome my new obstacle. Surely I could find the right trick to make this all instantly go away. I'm a problem solver. Endurance was for those who didn't know how to fix things. Rest? That sounded like giving up.

Though we live in a culture that glorifies the quick fix, I wonder if God doesn't sometimes allow adversity in our lives so we can learn to wait well. All those supplements that promised to zap me skinny and those exercise gizmos that guaranteed flat abs in five minutes a day failed me. But what if those investments were just lessons I paid three easy installments of $19.99 to learn?

As I age, I'm beginning to understand that every temporary solution I chase exposes a deeper longing inside of me. When I believe the marketers' ploys that a new car, more stylish clothes, or a made-over home will take away all my earthly struggles and shame, I buy into the lie. But true salvation is never found in the quick fix. The only One who can eliminate my pain wants me to find my rescue in Him alone.

One of my favorite verses in the Bible is Jonah 2:8. I know not many people choose a favorite verse from that book. In chapter 2, we read Jonah's conversation with God from inside the fish that swallowed him. I've been in uncomfortable situations before but never anything that compares to this. There's a ripe honesty to Jonah's words as he acknowledges God's greatness.

Verse 8 reads, "Those who cling to worthless idols turn away from God's love for them." Turns out my heart is just like Jonah's. I search for salvation in shiny packages. My heart is always eager to board an express train away from the struggle—which is exactly what idols offer. Idols promise instant results—heaven on earth if I follow their rules.

But the Bible tells a different story. Jonah is just one of several examples of people in the Bible who bought the lie that their way was better than God's. I guess my inclination to rescue myself isn't the internet's fault. Humans have been doing this since the beginning. Yet, what if the struggle is a gift?

Sanctification doesn't come in flashy packaging. Neither does it promise instant transformations. But God's sanctification process is a beautiful way to grow and strengthen our faith in the only One who can truly save us.

In Jonah 2:9, Jonah remembers that no matter how hard the path he's been called to, God will walk beside him. Here's what Jonah says: "But I will offer sacrifices to you with songs of praise, and I will fulfill all my vows. For my salvation comes from the LORD *alone*" (NLT, emphasis added). After this acknowledgment, the Lord commanded the fish to spit Jonah out.

Gaining weight is one of the most common complaints surrounding aging. We're aggravated that our metabolisms aren't what they used to be. We feel frustrated when health issues surface. When our energy disappears or the pounds creep on, it's tempting to buy a quick-fix ticket promising to take us away from the struggle.

But I wonder if the true answer to battling age-related health and weight issues isn't learning how to gain "wait." Scripture instructs us repeatedly to "wait" on the Lord. Lamentations 3:25 tells us, "The LORD is good to those who wait for him, to the soul who seeks him" (ESV). Isaiah 30:18 says, "Therefore the LORD waits to be gracious to you, and therefore he exalts himself to show mercy to you. For the LORD is a God of justice; blessed are all those who wait for him" (ESV). Or another one of my favorites, in Psalm 27:14, reads, "Wait for the LORD; be strong, and let your heart take courage; wait for the LORD!" (ESV).

We may not be waiting for the Lord to deliver us from a surrounding army ready to lay siege, but I know firsthand that when you wrestle your health, you're in a battle. We need courage and strength to wait for the Lord's deliverance.

As we wait we must remember that our hope is not in attaining optimal health or our ideal weight. Instead, we hope that someday true salvation will come and we'll be free from these earthly struggles. I am encouraged by Romans 8:18, which reminds us that "what we suffer now is nothing compared to the glory he will reveal to us later" (NLT).

Today I can be grateful that my ultimate hope is in heaven and in waiting on the Lord rather than being able to control my weight.

With this in mind, I wonder if Scripture doesn't give us the perfect prescription for a physically healthier life as well. Instead of chasing the quick fix and riding the on-again, off-again dieting roller coaster, what if we choose patience? What if we give our bodies the grace to change shape as we age? How would it look to pursue health goals slowly?

Taking the slower path is hard. We don't see the progress immediately and don't feel inspired to keep going. But the truth is, quick fixes make horrible saviors. Their power and encouragement always wear out. It is only the Lord who sustains us. As Isaiah 46:4 reminds us, he is the one who not only rescues us but carries us through: "I will be your God throughout your lifetime—until your hair is white with age. I made you, and I will care for you. I will carry you along and save you" (NLT).

All we have to do is gain wait.

Prayer

Dear Heavenly Father, I ask you to show me the areas of my life in which I need to gain wait. Whether it's a battle with

*my weight or with other aspects of my life where I've searched
for salvation from one of culture's quick-fix options, help me
put my trust, faith, and hope in you alone. Remind me to
wait on you, Lord, because you alone are my salvation!*

Aging Gratefully in Action

In what areas of your life is God helping you gain wait? What
have you been trying to cure with a quick fix? Make a list of
whatever comes to mind, and spend some time each day praying
over these areas and releasing them to the Father. Next, write the
words "Gain Wait" on a sticky note and put it on your Bible,
your mirror, your nightstand, or even your scale to help you remember to be patient in all your trials and as a reminder to wait
on the Lord for His rescue.

Wisdom Creases

Why Wrinkles Aren't the Enemy

Those who look to him are radiant, and
their faces shall never be ashamed.
PSALM 34:5 ESV

I've watched cosmetics commercials for years. I've religiously moisturized in a vain attempt to fend off the visible signs of aging. I've aggressively patted expensive potions around my eyes, mouth, and forehead. But why did no one caution me about what would happen to my skin, especially on my neck and below? If only someone had told me that pulling and pushing all over my face would have consequences.

Oh wait. That's right. She tried to tell me.

Her face is etched in my memory. Yes, it was wrinkled. But more so, it was sour as expired milk. Some people seem to frown when a smile is absent, but her resting expression was a scowl. She epitomized the grumpy neighbor. Yet she didn't live beside me. She worked in the office down the hall. I never even learned her name.

Fortunately I rarely saw her. That was on purpose. She constantly scolded my office mates and me, as if we were the rowdy children next door. She'd swing open her door and yell, "Keep it down—people are trying to work around here!"

Then one day, in the ladies' bathroom, she gave me beauty advice. Her eyes pierced my face through the mirror. She watched as I applied makeup. She turned up her nose and shook her head in disapproval before pronouncing judgment. "If you keep rubbing that hard, you'll look like me when you get older."

Her message was compelling. *I certainly don't want to look like her someday!* I thought.

But now I wonder. Was it really the wrinkles that I feared? It wasn't the appearance of her skin that made her difficult to be around. Neither was it the creases on her forehead that made me wait for the next elevator rather than ride up to the office with her. Instead, it was her disposition—her attitude. What troubled me about her wasn't that she looked old. No, the problem was much more than skin deep. It was that she lacked warmth, kindness, and any hint of love.

I think of 1 Corinthians 13, the Bible's famous love chapter. In verse 1, Paul tells us that without love we are a clanging symbol or a noisy gong. I wonder if we could rightly apply this passage to the condition of our skin. "If I am wrinkle-free but have not love . . ." "If I have a tight neck and can wear a stunning décolletage but have not love . . ." "If I have the pores of an angel and the elasticity of a sixteen-year-old but have not love . . ."

Smooth skin means nothing if your heart is rough.

The real problem isn't with getting older—it's with growing colder. Wrinkles and other physical signs of aging aren't to be feared. Instead, we must ensure we never age out of loving others well. That's when we become dour. That's when we start looking tired and old. You'll barely notice the so-called turkey neck on a woman who's always smiling.

The gospel of Luke introduces us to an elderly widow named Anna. I picture her a bit like Mother Teresa. Scripture tells us she never left the temple but stayed there day and night worshiping God and praying. When Mary and Joseph passed by with their infant, she knew that this baby was the Messiah. She immediately praised God and told everyone within earshot that the Savior had come! She knew the good news, and she spread it joyfully. I'm sure she had many wrinkles. Yet she didn't let aging spoil her attitude.

Remembering that we have the good news can revitalize us better than an antiaging skin cream. The daily active worship of God can keep our joy from sagging. And the beauty of seeing the gospel at work in our own lives and the lives of others can tighten our faith as nothing else can. Each of these practices will keep us from aging ugly.

> **The beauty of seeing the gospel at work in our own lives and the lives of others can tighten our faith.**

Now, I know you may still be thinking: *But still, what about my wrinkles? I'm not sure I like them.*

What if you consider your wrinkles the story lines of God's grace in your life? The more lines you have, the more grace you've been shown. Those creases and crinkles around your eyes and mouth? Perhaps they're symbols of all you've had to smile about.

There's a woman in the United Kingdom who is proud of the fact that she hasn't smiled in forty years. She's not leading a miserable life—instead she's determined to avoid wrinkles naturally.[4] As I read her story, I'm even more convinced. Expressing our pleasure is a part of our ability to enjoy life! It's far more important to show emotion than preserve a youthful look.

Scripture tells us there's a way to be beautiful, no matter the physical condition of our skin. Psalm 34:5 reads, "Those who look to him are radiant, and their faces shall never be ashamed" (ESV). Wrinkled or smooth. Creased or weathered. There's a path to a confident radiance that no bottle of wrinkle cream can offer.

Today I can be grateful for the wisdom creases. Like the prophetess Anna, I can know the good news and proclaim that no matter how old I look, I'm never too old to find joy in Him. I know wrinkles aren't the real enemy. Having a face that can't crack a warm smile is a far worse fate than crow's feet.

Prayer

Dear Heavenly Father, thank you that wrinkles can be signs of your grace. Help me to keep my focus on growing in love and worship no matter the condition of my skin. Teach me to see my wrinkles as story lines of your grace. Help me keep my heart's condition postured in praise to you.

Aging Gratefully in Action

If looking to God is the secret to radiance, what rituals do you have to become more radiant every day? Reading Scripture, spending time in prayer, and listening to worship music can cultivate a beauty that is unmatched by even the firmest skin. Keeping our eyes on the true source of beauty is the secret to ageless allure.

Crown of Grays

The Splendor of Hair-Color Freedom

Gray hair is a crown of splendor; it is
attained in the way of righteousness.
PROVERBS 16:31

Every six to eight weeks, I spend two and a half hours of my life sniffing chemicals while my hair gets pulled, teased, and wrapped in aluminum foil. After the first hour, I look like a creature from a sci-fi movie. Then I sit under a round heating hood that bakes my hairdresser's creation. It costs too much, and did I mention . . . the process takes hours?

So why do I do it? This is a question I've contemplated for years now. I'm not trying to cover grays. I don't have many yet. No, I grow strange-textured black hairs. Instead of a sprinkle of charming silver strands, these black wires spring from my scalp and refuse to be ruled by hair spray or gel. I was told it's okay to pluck them out. But I fear that someday that decision will have consequences. So instead I have them painted. And it's not a day of pampering at the spa. Whoever said blondes have more fun didn't know what kind of work it takes to stay that way.

Interestingly enough, coloring one's hair used to be a near-scandalous endeavor. Only starlets and harlots used hair dye. The practice was inappropriate for housewives or other women of high repute. The safety of the coloring products sparked some concern. But by and large, gray hair was an acceptable part of aging. There was no need to be ashamed that you were growing older. It was an understood part of life.

Go back a few hundred years and you'll find that graying hair was all the rage. In the 1700s, powdered hair was a symbol of status. Gray hair was synonymous with wisdom and righteousness, which is why most politicians chose to wear gray wigs or to powder their natural hair gray. It helped their credibility! But by 1943, a little company called Clairol had finally devised a "safe" home hair-color product. And they had one mission: to get more women coloring their hair at home.

Enter the gray scare. Advertising messages in the late 40s and 50s told women that gray hair "ruined romance." Another campaign encouraged women not to be left "buried under dull, drab" colorless hair. In the 1950s only 7 percent of women dyed their hair. But after a few more decades of messaging—such as the 1970s campaign reminding women they are "worth it" and the1980s tune about washing that gray right out of our hair—the needle moved. Now, up to 75 percent of women color their hair.[5] Men are told they're distinguished when the salt and pepper appear. But women can feel coerced to cover.

It's easy to see how we've been influenced by these messages. How the world defines beauty is vastly different from how the Word defines it. Scripture reminds us that the glory of aging is gray hair. Gray hair is a symbol of wisdom. There are at least eight places (depending on your translation) where gray hair is mentioned or used as a euphemism for aging.

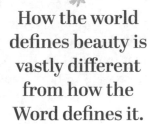

How the world defines beauty is vastly different from how the Word defines it.

The good news is, you have complete freedom in this arena. There's no biblical law that says you have to go gray. Neither is there a rule that says hair coloring is an abomination. Instead, you are free. Free to color and style your hair in the way you prefer.

But if you're like me, it's not permission to color that you need most. It's permission to let the gray show. Perhaps what we really need is affirmation to celebrate all that gray hair signifies.

One of my favorite verses about going gray is Proverbs 16:31: "Gray hair is a crown of glory; it is gained by living a godly life" (NLT). The wisest man who ever lived calls gray hair a crown, not a curse. When you think of a crown, you normally think of a winner, not a loser. It's amazing how different this picture is from the one painted by the hair-color ads.

Ironically, isn't our "crown of glory" part of the reason why we color? Who doesn't want to be a winner? Miss America wears a crown, and so did the ancient Olympians. Kings, queens, and other royalty also wear these symbols of their status. It's as if Solomon knew that we'd need to see our hair pigment changing as a reward instead of a punishment.

Other Scriptures assure us that a crown of grays is certainly a good thing biblically. In Proverbs 12:4, we read that an excellent wife is the crown of her husband. And in Proverbs 4:9, we see that wisdom will place a beautiful garland or a crown of beauty on your head. Again, wearing a crown is an honor that not all receive.

It's a bit of a tragedy that gray hair is no longer lauded as a trophy. Perhaps it's just more evidence that our culture and the Bible view aging vastly different. **But today I can be grateful that graying hair is a prize and not a punishment.** I can see the reward and the beauty of God's promise to those of us who are feeling our age. In Isaiah 46:4–5, God makes His people a promise: "Even when you're old, I'll take care of you. Even when your hair turns gray, I'll support you. I made you and will continue to care for you" (GW).

Prayer

Dear Heavenly Father, please help me to see my aging hair as a part of your grace to me. Help me to hold tight to Scripture's view of aging and not buy into culture's narrative that I will age out of relevance unless I strive to maintain my youthful appearance. Help me to see aging the way you do.

Aging Gratefully in Action

Do you think about graying hair as splendid? It's an interesting exercise to stop and think about how our views of beauty have been deeply impacted by marketing messages over the last hundred years. Of course, we are completely free to color if that's what we prefer. But I wonder how our own perspectives on aging would change if we started complimenting those who have let their crowns go gray. Acknowledging gray hair as beautiful can help your heart believe that God's beauty salon specializes not in covering grays but in crowning them.

Learning Who's Really in Control

The Sweet Surrender of Knowing Who's Boss

She is clothed with strength and dignity, and
she laughs without fear of the future.
PROVERBS 31:25 NLT

From my office, I heard my husband directing his troops
(our teens) to help with some household chores while I
wrote. His instructions: fold this basket of towels. There
was no follow-up tutorial on how to fold the towels, no directions clarifying how to transform a rectangle into a closet-
friendly shape. In fact, I heard no conversation at all. That
signaled that folding was happening without instruction.

Now that we've gotten to know each other a bit, I have a
question for you. How long would it take you to go see if they
were folding the towels properly?

I was seconds away from sprinting into that room to offer

my popular TED Talk: "Towel Folding for a Better Tomorrow." But then I sat back down and determined it didn't really matter. Back to writing.

Oh no! Someone just commented they're all different sizes. I ready myself for a rescue mission. But again I stay seated. The lesson I'm learning: It's okay to surrender control.

You may read this and think, *Who cares about towel folding?* Or you may read this and wonder what kind of insane person *doesn't* get up and make sure the towels are folded properly. Maybe you find yourself somewhere on the spectrum between towel obstinance and oblivion. If correct folding isn't your hang-up, perhaps it's loading the dishwasher or the way your bed is made. Or maybe you can't pinpoint one particular thing you like done "right" because you're that special breed of perfectionist who believes everything should be done right. (Been there.)

The older I get, the more I'm learning to understand my limits. Which is a blessing in the arenas of perfectionism and control. I can finally see that, after all these years, perhaps I didn't have as much control as I thought I did. Who was I fooling? I can't even control my fifteen-pound dog when a package gets delivered to the front door.

Control seemed to serve me well in my work. My ability to walk into a room and list everything wrong with it was helpful to employers expecting a successful gala. Adherence to tight timelines and strict standards led to career success.

But in relationships, my controlling nature was not an asset. The groomsmen at our wedding mocked my minute-by-minute schedule for their entire weekend. The volunteers on my team at church didn't enjoy my constant check-ins on their progress. And apparently my husband and teenagers feel more loved when I don't criticize their appearance as if they're preparing to meet the paparazzi.

Control feels suffocating to the one on the receiving end.

Healthy relationships require trust, understanding, and a splash of freedom. We controllers forget to treat ourselves and others with the same dose of grace that God imparts. By fixating on the flaws, we miss out on our opportunity to savor the good and feel grateful for it.

The book of James contains many truths for daily living and just may hold the secret to surrendering control. Look at James 1:2–4:

> Count it all joy, my brothers, when you meet trials
> of various kinds, for you know that the testing of
> your faith produces steadfastness. And let steadfast-
> ness have its full effect, that you may be perfect and
> complete, lacking in nothing. (ESV)

Today I noticed a little word in this passage that has immense meaning for women like me who enjoy details and precision. The word is "let." Do you see it there? "Let steadfastness have its full effect."

To "let" something happen, we have to surrender control. Growing in maturity requires this. We may have to wave the white flag with our families or friends, allowing relationships to change in seasons as God designed. We may have to surrender our jobs, careers, or even our spouse's career to the God we know will provide. Or we may have to yield rebellious adult children to the care of the God who loves them even more than we do. There are many things in life that may not match our plan, but there is freedom when we learn to "let."

Not knowing what God has planned next? That feels uncertain and risky. And that makes me afraid. That's when control whispers its lie that it all depends on me. Make a plan. Fix it. Don't miss a single detail. But that burden is crushing and can damage both our relationships and our health.

Fear chants, "If it's going to be, it's up to me," then panics in the face of unforeseen change. But faith and trust sing songs of surrender.

Our culture offers complimentary lessons on being self-made, as if being in control of one's life is worthy of a scout's merit badge. But God didn't design us to hold responsibility for our own provision. And He's certainly never asked us to pretend we have His power and omnipotence while we make believe that we're supreme rulers of our domains.

Faith and trust sing songs of surrender.

The Bible teaches that God is in control. His strength is made perfect not in my planning but in my weakness. When I see there's only one boss, I find the freedom to live and enjoy life.

The older I get, the more I see the reality of my future. Even if I think I can handle it all alone now, someday I will need to lean on others. I see the futility and hardship of building a life where it all depends on me. Aging's path always leads us away from independence. We can learn to surrender the reins now or someday have them taken from us. I think of coaching clients who have spent a lifetime overexercising only to face injuries in midlife that permanently change their physical capabilities.

I long to be a woman who can smile in the face of the future because I know that God's got it. I want to look back on my life and be grateful as I recognize that He was in control all along. All those times when I believed I was running the show, I was more like the three-year-old helping her mom bake. The preschooler claims the achievement when the cookies come out of the oven, but everyone knows who really did the work.

Today I can be grateful for—especially in the areas I don't want to let go—to the God who cares. I don't have to amp up my inner control freak to know I'll be safe. God loves me and wants me to trust Him. When I think ahead to the future, God's promise is that I have nothing to fear. If He cares about the birds and the flowers, how much more will He provide for me?

Even if the towels are folded wrong.

Prayer

Dear Heavenly Father, thank you that you are in control. Thank you that, like the woman of great faith from Proverbs 31, I can smile as I think about what's ahead because I know you hold it all—my worries, my days, and even my body—in your hands. Help me ease up on the reins as I age, knowing that I can always feel safe in the palm of your hand.

Aging Gratefully in Action

Let's be honest—control doesn't look good on anyone. Often motivated by fear, control robs us of the peace and joy God intends when we put our trust in Him. Control pushes people away from us instead of drawing them close. When our offer is "my way or the highway," even the compliant want to run in the other direction. Take an inventory today of the areas of your life where you may be clinging to control. Add these to your prayer list, and ask God daily to help you through the process of surrender.

The Hottest Person I Know

Menopause and Midlife Change

Let perseverance finish its work so that you may be
mature and complete, not lacking anything.
JAMES 1:4

It's ironic how we spend so much of our youth trying to
be hotter. Then sometime between forty and sixty, hotness
hits us smack between the eyes in a way we never desired.
There's no warning. One minute I'm living my life. The next,
I'm either already sweating through my shirt or stressed that the
next hot flash awaits the most inopportune time to surprise me.
My friend Lindsey calls this phenomenon "personal summers."
It sounds like an exotic personal getaway to somewhere warm.
Yet most women I know don't see menopause as a vacation.
Hormones are real.

In addition to my ability to heat up faster than my Keurig, I now have phenomenal emotional diversity. I can be happy, sad, angry, and teary-eyed within the same hour. I'm an equal-opportunity emoter. I can't remember if I took my pills this morning, yet I am acutely aware of who ate the last brownie. The uncertainty of what's happening inside takes me back to being fourteen again. Only it's even more confusing this time because I thought I'd figured my body out.

Meno*pause*. Of course, it's not really a pause. It's a full stop. An ending. It's a marking of maturity. We talk about menopause as if it's a season, but technically we're suffering through perimenopause before and postmenopause after the menopause milestone. As soon as you've gone without a period for twelve months, you've hit menopause. But, you're not just paused—you're finished with a significant season of your journey as a woman.

In many ways, I'll celebrate the stop. The ability to wear white pants without regard and not having a beach vacation dampened by a visit from "Aunt Flo" . . . These will be the prizes of the postmeno me.

And yet with the full stop comes the in-your-face reality of aging. There's no more pretending like I'm not getting older. The change of life enters stage right and makes me wonder what's left.

When the estrogen turns down, what really turns up? Is it just the physical changes that bog us down, or is it something more? Could it be that what bothers us most about the pause is the feeling that we've lost control over our bodies?

I'd finally started to figure out my body. Though teen years and pregnancies rendered my body an unpredictable nuisance, I had finally gained a new sense of peace with my monthly fluctuations. Then boom! It goes rogue. Off grid. Just when I'd learned to dance to the rhythm of womanhood, the change of life seized me like a prisoner of hormonal war. Other types of maturity don't follow a neat, step-by-step process. I guess I shouldn't expect anything different from my body's maturing process.

If you're like me, any perceived chaos throws me into fix-it mode. I hope that somehow if I do everything right, I can avoid the symptoms of a changing body. By fighting with everything I've got, I try to beat it. Yet I wonder if that doesn't just make menopause worse. What if the best way to thrive during the change requires us to declare peace, not war.

When it comes to menopause, I recently heard a doctor talking about how meditation helped her more than medication. The daily practice of quiet and calmness grounded her emotionally, mentally, and physically. Though her perspective wasn't that of a Christ-follower, I couldn't help but see how her advice aligns with God's. Meditation has spiritual benefits when combined with Scripture and prayer. While we may long for freedom from the symptoms of the change, what we really need is more peace. And the best way to get peace in the pause is to meditate and pray.

Psalm 1:2 tells us that the one who is blessed delights in the law

> **The best way to get peace in the pause is to meditate and pray.**

of the Lord and "meditates on his law day and night." Even if you went through the change of life years ago, meditating on Scripture is a helpful practice for relaxing our minds and our bodies. Consider how particular verses hold the power to encourage, uplift, and minister to you in other circumstances. Certainly, in the midst of the hormonal storm of menopause, meditating on God's Word can have this same calming effect. When our hearts are at peace, our bodies can follow suit.

Of course, finding peace is sometimes a struggle in and of itself. But Isaiah 26:3 reminds, "You will keep in perfect peace those whose minds are steadfast, because they trust in you."

There's no better expression of our trust in God than prayer. Taking all our concerns to Him demonstrates that He is the one in whom we've placed our trust.

The apostle Paul further encourages us that prayer is the place that will alleviate our worries, including the physical changes we endure as we age. A familiar passage in 1 Thessalonians 5:16–18 reads, "Rejoice always, pray without ceasing, give thanks in all circumstances; for this is the will of God in Christ Jesus for you" (ESV).

Let's not forget that all this meditation could be preparation for what God has in store next in our lives. Yes, God can and does use postmenopausal women for His glory. I could list the matriarchs of the faith—both ancient and modern—who have accomplished extraordinary things for God's kingdom after fifty, sixty, or older. Yet I don't think believing God can do great things with our lives is where we get stuck. Instead, it's in allowing Him to. He's not finished with us yet.

Today I can be grateful that meditating on God's Word assures me that my life hasn't passed like a hot flash. Though menopause marks the end of a season, I'm a work in progress as I reach not just physical maturity but spiritual maturity when I meditate on His truth and savor His peace.

Prayer

Dear Heavenly Father, help me to persevere. Give me the grace to handle the physical and emotional changes that accompany menopause. Help me to make peace with my changing life by staying connected to you through meditating on Scripture and praying. Use this time to grow and prepare me so I can be used for your mission and purpose.

Aging Gratefully in Action

As estrogen powers down, consider what your body needs to power up. Many menopause experts agree that stress management—such as prayer and meditation, taking walks or baths, or listening to calming music—can help symptom management when hormones feel out of control. Carve out quiet time to spend with the Lord each morning so you can feel His peace even when your body feels at war.

Dressing Your Age

Scripture's Suggestion for Dressing Well as You Age

Put on then, as God's chosen ones, holy and beloved,
compassionate hearts, kindness, humility, meekness,
and patience, bearing with one another and, if one has
a complaint against another, forgiving each other; as
the Lord has forgiven you, so you also must forgive.
COLOSSIANS 3:12–13 ESV

As a teen, I remember shopping with my mom and wondering why she always chose clothing from the old ladies section. Surely she could find something more fashionable in juniors. Why did she prefer these clothes to what was in style?

Now, I get it. When you have photographs of yourself wearing puff sleeves to your tenth-grade piano recital, it's a leap to put them on again at fifty. Some can and do, and I admire them for their fashion courage. But for others—like me—it's a struggle to know how to dress our age without feeling like we're trying to squeeze an old body into young clothes. Frankly, the thought of wearing prairie dresses or floral rompers with lace collars—again—makes me cringe.

Though Scripture doesn't tell us what fashions to wear, it does tell us how to dress. It's interesting that God uses the language of clothing as the context to instruct and encourage His people with what will look best on them.

Kindness, humility, patience, and meekness—what a list! This fashion advice runs contrary to the images of beauty projected around us: to get noticed, be bold, be proud, and be demanding. But God tells us the best way to be beautifully attired is to wear these virtues listed in Colossians.

In the style world, image is everything. But what if we embraced the fashion advice of the One in whose image we were made? The image we most need to project is one that's modeled after Him instead of in magazines.

What makes a woman beautiful over forty, over fifty, and beyond? It's not her ability to pull off outfits designed for teenagers. Instead, it's how she dresses in kindness, humility, patience, and meekness.

What do all of these virtues have in common? They're about putting others first. Thinking of others before ourselves. Not being afraid of second, third, or last place. Waiting on others or, in some cases, watching others accomplish or attain things that are still on our to-do lists.

Culture teaches that if you put yourself first, you'll reach the top. It preaches that since you've reached midlife, you finally have the time to make *you* a priority—as if now's your chance to focus on becoming the best version of yourself.

But what if the best way to be more beautiful in midlife is to take the focus off of ourselves and serve others, like Jesus did. Wearing humility, gentleness, and peace will always be age appropriate. Loving others is a flattering style on every body.

If you picture the people who have cared for you well, chances are you don't picture the clothes they wore. Instead, you see the beauty of their hearts.

This isn't the only passage in the New Testament that offers fashion advice. Peter adds this insight in 1 Peter 3:3–4: "Don't be concerned about the outward beauty of fancy hairstyles, expensive jewelry, or beautiful clothes. You should clothe yourselves instead with the beauty that comes from within, the unfading beauty of a gentle and quiet spirit, which is so precious to God" (NLT).

> **By putting on patience, kindness, meekness, and humility, I can confidently wear what never goes out of fashion.**

Perhaps the best news is, no matter how we feel about our bodies, how they're aging, or the fashion trends, we can always exude style when we follow Scripture's wisdom for dressing our age.

Today I can be grateful that God's wardrobe recommendations free me to look truly beautiful at any age. They don't require me to try to recapture my youth or keep the body of a twentysomething. Instead, by putting on patience, kindness, meekness, and humility, I can confidently wear what never goes out of fashion.

Prayer

Dear Heavenly Father, help me to let go of my old definitions of style that are about capturing the attention and affection of others. Instead, help me to be stylish in ways that matter for eternity.

Aging Gratefully in Action

Scripture's mandate is clear. We are to put on kindness, humility, patience, and meekness as we relate to and love others well. Becoming fashionable in this way starts by becoming intentional about noticing others. Instead of walking into a room wondering what others are thinking about you, shift your focus and ask, "How can I love them well?" Spot one woman who looks like she needs a friend and engage in conversation. Ask another how you can pray for her and then follow up with a note or email. You'll be amazed at how seeking ways to encourage others offers freedom from common insecurities like worrying about our clothes.

Why Did I Pick Up My Phone?

Encouragement for Aging Brains

Is not wisdom found among the aged? Does
not long life bring understanding?
JOB 12:12

hat's the temperature going to be tomorrow? I pick up
my phone, but instead of opening the weather app, I
check my email. I scroll social media. I read a linked
article. Then I'm shopping on Amazon. Before I know it, thirty
minutes have passed. I close my phone with this nagging feeling
that I've forgotten something. *Oh yes, the weather.*

I open it again, determined not to fall into the same pit of
forgetfulness. But a text message comes through. I reply, then
open my email. Soon I'm back to texting. And I still don't know
if I need a jacket tomorrow.

I'd like to blame it on the device—I know it's secretly

designed to rewire neural pathways. Yet I wonder: Could my brain be aging too?

I did a little research. Turns out our brains start to shrink in our thirties and forties. By age sixty the shrinkage rate increases even more. According to scientists, it's not just the appearance of our bodies that changes in midlife. Our brains look different too.[6] Aging doesn't miss a thing, does it?

But there's good news. Though our minds delete some details, aging allows our brains to get better at seeing the big picture. I accidentally proved this to be true when I proudly handed the grocery store clerk a coupon for ten dollars off. She had a puzzled look on her face, so I thought I'd help her out. "It expires on the twentieth. Today's only the nineteenth!" I proudly exclaimed. She looked at the coupon and then back at me. "Yes, ma'am, but this was for last month."

Oops. My face flushed. A man in line behind me who was old enough to be my father shot me a compassionate look. *So I couldn't remember what month it was? Big deal.* Years ago, the embarrassment (and the missed opportunity for savings) would have weighed me down like my minivan after a Costco run. But my perspective is maturing. We needed the groceries anyway. There was no shame in buying them, even without the coupon. It's okay that I made a mistake in front of the whole line. I'm only human.

Although my aging brain may not remember what month it is, that doesn't mean it's not working as it should. Perhaps these shifts allow us to focus on what's truly important in midlife. What if my aging brain has learned to tune out superfluous details in order to zero in on who and what life is about?

Job 12:12 reads, "Is not wisdom found among the aged? Does not long life bring understanding?" Just because I'm repeating stories or struggling to remember that one item I stopped at the store to grab doesn't mean my brain is failing.

The belief that the opinions and thought processes of the young are superior to those of the old is a relatively new cultural sensation. Elders used to be valued members of their communities. When did we buy the lie that an old brain is a useless brain?

Sure, my brain is changing. But what if, like the rest of my body, there's tremendous grace in that? Perhaps brain changes in midlife help us better follow Scripture's commands about our thought lives. Could it be that a more mature brain is better equipped to love others well or more adept to taking thoughts captive, like Paul urges us to do in 2 Corinthians 10:5?

Philippians 4:8 is a verse I memorized in the third grade. We recited it before our Missionettes program at church every Wednesday night. "And now, dear brothers and sisters, one final thing. Fix your thoughts on what is true, and honorable, and right, and pure, and lovely, and admirable. Think about things that are excellent and worthy of praise" (NLT).

Back then I couldn't fully appreciate its instruction. Now I see it. Wrong thoughts can destroy us. Obsessive spirals, fear-laden ruminations, imagining the worst with only crumbs of evidence—these patterns steal our peace. Where our mind goes, our hearts and bodies will follow. What we think about determines what we believe, and what we believe determines what we do. And all of that starts in the brain. Our thought lives are extremely important.

Sure, I'm of the age where my soundtrack of wrong thoughts still plays on a cassette tape instead of a digital device. But that doesn't mean I'm too old to change it. Instead, I can just hold down the Record and Play buttons at the same time and tape right over that wrong thinking with the Bible's list of what to dwell on.

Yes, an aging brain can present daily obstacles—like when I'm staring at a woman I've known for years and suddenly have no idea what her name is. But perhaps these situations are part of my sanctification. I can stop obsessing over getting everything right and instead train my thoughts to align with God's truth. Offering a sincere "I'm so sorry—my brain is not allowing me access to the file with your name in it right now. It's a password problem" can help add humor to those brain glitches we all experience.

Today I am grateful that aging brains can flourish with wisdom and understanding. Now that I'm older, perhaps my ability to better see the big picture of God's grace will also make it easier to focus on what's healthy, helpful, and most important. I can choose to cultivate a healthy thought life no matter my age.

Prayer

Dear Heavenly Father, help my aging brain focus on what is true, holy, and right. Help me to focus my thoughts on things that are excellent and worthy of praise instead of thoughts that want to defeat me. Continue to show me the big picture of your grace and truth.

Aging Gratefully in Action

Consider posting Philippians 4:8 in places where you can see it all day so it can become the filter through which you test your thoughts to see if they are true, holy, pure, lovely, and admirable. Create an image with the verse on it and make it your home screen on your phone. Write it out and tape it to your bathroom mirror. According to doctors, the process of renewing our minds requires the

You're never too old to change your thinking.

creation of new neural pathways.[7] It's amazing how this matches Scripture's teaching to take thoughts captive and intentionally dwell on healthier and holier truths. You're never too old to change your thinking.

Can God Still Use Me?

You Are Never Too Late for His Purpose

Now faith is confidence in what we hope for
and assurance about what we do not see.
HEBREWS 11:1

Picture this. You're making big plans for your ninetieth birthday. You've had a full life, but there's one thing you haven't experienced yet. Something you've always desired—to have a baby. Forget peeing on a stick. God sends a messenger to tell you that it's happening. Your dream is going to come true! Next year at this time, you'll be holding a newborn. How do you feel?

My answer: terrified.

Isn't that too old to have a baby? Isn't that too old to be a mother? What kind of mom could I be in between doctor's visits for arthritis flare-ups and my afternoon naps? Scripture tells us that Sarah laughed. I'm afraid I would have argued.

"Oh, thanks so much, God. Yes. It's my dream. But I don't

think I'm ready for it now. I was ready decades ago. It feels like you may have missed the window."

Most of us will never face the prospect of pregnancy past fifty. Yet I wonder if there isn't another lesson we can learn from Sarah. Perhaps our takeaway from her story could be that we're never too old to fulfill God's purpose for our lives.

Purpose is an overused word that can feel ambiguous. There are one hundred different ways you could live on purpose every day. Sometimes the cliché "find your purpose" can feel like scavenging for lost treasure in the rain forest. *Find my purpose? Do they sell those at Target?*

Culturally we're taught that successful people peak at thirty-five and float out of relevance somewhere around sixty. Exceptions to this rule make the list of people who peaked late. American folk artist Grandma Moses started painting at seventy-seven years old. Vera Wang didn't start designing clothes until she was thirty-nine. We're to be inspired by these "exceptions" while understanding that most people make their mark while they're young.

But that's not God's design. The Bible shows us stories about people like Sarah and Moses—stories of men and women of all ages and abilities chosen to accomplish His purpose. When we believe that purpose is only for the young, we conflate culture's ideas about success, status, productivity, and profits with the teaching of God's Word.

Scripture's definition of purpose is both broader and yet, somehow, more specific. Part of our purpose is to know God and tell others about Him. We were created to worship and be in relationship with our Creator, our loving heavenly Father. Every day, no matter my age or mobility, I can live out this purpose. There's no ambiguity here.

Beyond this, God created each of us to do something in His kingdom. We have been given spiritual gifts—talents, passions, personalities, and stories that uniquely equip us to play a role in

His kingdom now and for all eternity. Everyone who calls Jesus "Lord" plays a part in the church body. First Corinthians 12 and Ephesians 4:11–16 bring clarification to the roles He calls us to within a community of believers.

At age ninety, Sarah experienced a lifelong dream fulfilled. She became the mother of a people. Entire generations, consecrated to God, would follow from this one son. Yet I wonder if Sarah lived most of her life feeling unfulfilled. She had the promise of purpose but not the practice. As we walk through midlife, could this be an essential lesson for us to learn now, decades before we've reached Sarah's age?

In Genesis 17:16, God tells Abraham that He's changing his wife's name and that He will bless her. In fact, He repeats that last part twice: "I will bless her, and moreover, I will give you a son by her. I will bless her, and she shall become nations; kings of peoples shall come from her" (ESV).

Sarah's blessing comes both in practice and in promise. She is blessed with the baby, but she's also blessed beyond the baby. God sees her. He knows her. He's chosen her for this specific mission.

The same is true for us. Though we may not have a Scripture verse with our name in it, God's promise to us is the same. He loves us. He sees us. He knows us. And He's chosen us for a specific mission. This is the promise.

The practice of this mission is even more fun. We have the freedom to figure out how we were wired and what gifts and talents we can use to serve. Discovering our "why" makes us feel alive! You may find that in this season of life you have more resources to serve in ways that weren't possible in your younger years. God's greatest aspiration for our lives is not that we'd reach retirement and, as John Piper famously teaches, devote our lives to collecting seashells.[8] What if we pressed forward with anticipation for the next assignment on our mission?

Midlife isn't the wind-down of a purpose-driven life. It's the wind-up. What dreams has God put on your heart? What gifts has he given you that you've not yet used? Now that we have more freedom, maturity, and life experience, there are many ways we can put our purpose into practice.

Every week I have the opportunity to coach women who've spent significant portions of their lives battling their size, shape, or other aspects of their bodies they were sure needed to change. As we work together, this concept of purpose consistently surfaces. Many who battle body image haven't understood how God made us to be more than just bodies. Their identities have been so caught up in the mission of body transformation that their kingdom purpose has felt lost. The concept of practicing their purpose frees them to feel valuable, useful, and blessed in a way they've never before experienced.

Of course, the greatest fulfillment of our purpose comes in the promise that someday we will experience the consummation of our relationship with Jesus. Though someday we'll meet Him face-to-face, we will also feel flashes of this promise here as we understand and carry out what it is we've been created to do.

It can feel scary to wonder if you've found what you were called to and created for. Maybe you, like Sarah, felt called to a specific purpose but put that dream out to pasture because you felt you'd missed your prime. Remember, you're never too old for God to use you.

Today I can be grateful that God has a purpose for my life in every season. I'll never age out of my ability to accomplish great things for God's kingdom. I can practice His purpose daily by devoting myself to growing in my relationship with Him.

Prayer

Dear Heavenly Father, thank you that it's never too late for me to discover my purpose. Lead and direct me to the purpose you have planned for me in practice. Meanwhile, Lord, remind me that the greatest promise I have is that someday I'll see you. Help me prepare for that day by intentionally building my relationship with you now.

Aging Gratefully in Action

Do you know what God wired you to do? Have you taken a spiritual gifts test to see what gifts He's given you to be used within the body of Christ? Romans 12:6–8 and 1 Corinthians 12:8–10 each hold lists of gifts God has given every believer. If you don't know your gifts, take a free spiritual gifts assessment online and explore how you can use your gifts for God's kingdom here on earth. Then write a list of areas in which you enjoy serving and tasks that you are good at, and ask God to show you how He wants to use these gifts in your church and community. A beautiful life is one lived on purpose for God's glory.

Day 17

Mission Accomplice

Partnering with God on His Mission for Your Life

Many are the plans in a person's heart, but it
is the LORD's purpose that prevails.
PROVERBS 19:21

I couldn't wait to turn thirty. I spent my twenties trying to prove my maturity and demonstrate that I had enough know-how to do the jobs I'd been given. I wearied of people questioning my age. I was eager to proudly tell people I was "in my thirties."

Twenty-nine sounded young. But thirty? That sounded old. Experienced. Qualified. How foolish that seems now. Yet, whether we're thirty, sixty, or ninety, I wonder if it isn't our bent to question our own qualifications as we ponder what God created us to do.

What is your mission—do you know? It doesn't have to be something big and audacious. In fact, often the more miraculous missions are small and unseen. What if the difference you make in just one person's life is the exact mission for which God created you?

99

Purpose is about partnership and promise. Your first mission is to continue to grow in the knowledge of your Savior. Author Tim Challies tells the story of an older woman who explained she was no longer reading the Bible to understand how to live. She was reading the Bible to get to know God better because she knew she'd meet Him soon.[9]

It's difficult to live in the tension of having a glorious destiny in heaven and yet, still having work to do here on earth. Though I'm anxious to meet Jesus someday, I'm also hopeful I have several decades left here. But, I'm not thirty anymore. Time isn't as infinite as I once believed.

Which I guess is why there's a rush at midlife to make plans and do all those things we once only dreamed of. Social media posts boast of check marks on bucket lists. *They* went on vacation to Alaska. *They* took that cruise through Europe. *They* journeyed to the Holy Land. Some sit down to write novels. Others go on adventures. Why the hurry at midlife to do things we've only once dreamed of? Feeling like time is fleeting ensues urgency. We're willing to spend more time and money on what's important to us because we may never have the chance again. We long to make a mark by doing something meaningful.

But shouldn't our real sense of urgency be about accomplishing what God has created us to do? At this stage we're often not confined to a bed, looking back on our lives, wondering *what if* from a point of no return. Rather, we still have time, capacity, energy, and often resources to get busy. We're not done yet. Instead of mission accomplished, what if we postured ourselves in such a way where we say to God, "I'll be your mission accomplice."

> **What if we postured ourselves in such a way where we say to God, "I'll be your mission accomplice."**

Imposter syndrome may creep in and tell you that you're not good enough to do that. Culture's glorification of youth might make you feel too old to start something new. But remember, you're not on this mission alone. You have an accomplice.

Though the most common definitions of this word have to do with criminal activity, the origins of the word paint a more elaborate picture of what it means to have an accomplice. The Latin origin *complicare* means "to involve, fold, or weave together with someone." What a beautiful illustration of what happens when we surrender our lives to God's purpose and plans.

I'm not an outstanding baker, but I've spent some quality time in the kitchen turning butter, sugar, eggs, and flour into cookies or cakes. You fold the dry ingredients into the melted butter and eggs until you no longer see the separation between the two. You have something new—a delicious batter. *First dibs on licking the spoon!*

When we partner with our great accomplice, He folds together a beautiful mixture of our divine purpose. As you explore what gifts God has given you, how He's wired you, and what passions He's placed inside you, it's amazing to see how He uses your willing heart to turn His purpose into something you could never have imagined for yourself.

As we continue to walk in this purpose, soon it becomes clear that the path is one we could not have forged for ourselves. We no longer see where our work stops and God's work begins. Our mission becomes interwoven with divine threads that define the tapestry.

Culture preaches that satisfaction and joy are found in recognizing your own greatness. However, when you walk in God's purpose for your life, it's not your own glory you recognize, but His. Perhaps you've already experienced this amazing display of God's goodness. Maybe you've felt God's presence as you praised Him for orchestrating opportunities or opening doors you could have never cracked open yourself.

Today I can be grateful that God is my mission accomplice. He hasn't set me on a course toward finding my purpose without Him. He knows exactly where I'm at in my life. He knows who I've become, how I'm wired and gifted. He has a purpose for me for the remainder of my days. With God, nothing He's called me to is impossible (Luke 1:37).

Prayer

Dear Heavenly Father, show me what mission you have for me to partner with you and accomplish. Help me to live courageously as your mission accomplice. Keep my eyes focused on you as the ultimate quencher of my midlife thirst for meaning, relevance, and purpose.

Aging Gratefully in Action

As you explore your spiritual gifts and areas in which God may have equipped you to serve your local church and community, remember that the best way to find a place to serve is to volunteer. In some cases, you may not know fully how you've been equipped to serve until you take a few steps of faith and try it out. Does God keep bringing a certain ministry to mind? Or is there an expressed need at your church that always seems to go unfilled? Sometimes we don't know which roles are a great fit until we try them on.

Who Stole My Energy?

Using Time Wisely

> I will restore to you the years that the swarming
> locust has eaten, the hopper, the destroyer, and the
> cutter, my great army, which I sent among you.
> JOEL 2:25

It happened again. I heard the question and knew what my answer should be. Yet as my soul screamed "No," my mouth said, "Sure, I can do that."

What? No! I can't do that. I shouldn't do that. I'm overcommitted in one hundred different ways. That "little" task I agreed to may seem insignificant, but in the scheme of my life, too many yeses have stolen my energy.

You see, I signed up to bring cookie bars. Two dozen of them. I perused the sign-up sheet, secretly calculating what would be the quickest to make. The coordinator did backpedal—"You're so busy that you don't have to bring anything"—but instead of hearing permission to come without contributing, I internalized a dare.

Yet when the time came to make good on my sign-up, my energy ran out. After a packed day, I sat down for a two-minute reprieve on the couch. It was almost 9:00 p.m. As I thought through the day to come, I reached a crossroads. Bed or bars?

Bed won. No contest. I mentally pledged to alternative plans. Maybe I could get everyone up early and go to the store on the way? But deep down I knew I couldn't keep that promise either.

So I arrived without my bars. Apparently, I wasn't the only one facing a cookie-commitment predicament. As I assessed the buffet, it looked a little light—others had chosen bed over baking too. I sensed the coordinator's frustration. She made announcements about everyone only taking two treats. Then came the shame I placed on myself. *You should have done better.*

What followed was a brand-new sensation. The guilt wave came, but I let it crest and fade without drowning me. A decade ago one look at that snack table would have sent me sprinting to the supermarket. Or I would've spent fifteen minutes explaining the minutia of my life until the coordinator was convinced that it really was unreasonable for me to bring bars. That day I felt none of that pressure. Instead, I celebrated a victory in *almost* saying no.

Of course, how much wiser would it have been if I had actually said no from the start? I've been the one holding the sign-up sheet and the pen too many times. It's not nice to leave leaders in a lurch. Yet for me, this snack fail offered an opportunity for growth, a chance to experience my own humanness and accept grace when life leads to letting others down.

The older I get, the more I realize that my energy is a precious commodity. For decades I've used it as if it'd never run out. From "I'll make two dozen" to "Sure, I can watch your kids," the ways I've overcommitted through the decades are numerous. Now I'm learning (slowly, it seems) the importance of saving my yeses for the things that the Lord has actually called me to.

Though some days it feels like I can do all the things (or try to), I know it's best for my body to slow down. I've walked through near adrenal fatigue thanks to decades of overworking and overdoing. I see now how much of my motivation wasn't about serving Jesus. I chose to overdo and overwork for the approval of others.

I'm reminded of the story of the boy with the two loaves of bread and the five tiny fish. Jesus took his little lunch and turned it into an all-you-can-eat buffet that fed more than five thousand people. Though the story is in all four gospels, only the book of John acknowledges the owner of the lunch box.

In John 6:11, we read that after Jesus took the loaves and fish, he gave thanks and distributed them. The Scripture tells us that everyone ate until they were satisfied. In the end they filled twelve baskets with leftover pieces of those original five loaves. It was a miracle. Only Jesus could stretch a sandwich into a smorgasbord.

Could it be that one of the secret gifts of aging is that as our bodies slow, we realize that we no longer have the capacity to do all the things all the time? I wonder if the lesson Jesus demonstrates is that when we spend our energy on the activities He has called us to, He expands it. With His blessing and calling, our capacity swells. We feel invigorated and alive.

> **With His blessing and calling, our capacity swells.**

Yet when we try to do it all in our own strength and spend energy on missions we were never commissioned for, the crash may take days of recovery. When I was younger, I could just take a nap and feel better. But now, energy depletion aches everywhere. Wasting time when I'm careless with my commitments renders me useless to those who actually need me. Plus it robs others, who may be equipped and ready for that mission, from taking their intended role.

Growing up, whenever seasons of struggle persisted, my mom would always pray a verse from Joel 2. The passage is about judgment coming to the land of Judah. But it's also about what would happen if the people repented and turned from their evil ways. Part of the blessing of restoration is God's promise to "restore to you the years that the swarming locust has eaten" (Joel 2:25 ESV).

English theologian and preacher Charles Spurgeon explains how the locust really didn't have the ability to eat time. Instead, the locust had eaten the fruits of the Israelites' labor during that time. Spurgeon explains, "You cannot have back your time; but there is a strange and wonderful way in which God can give you back the wasted blessings, the unripened fruits of years over which you mourned."[10]

I wonder how many fruit-filled opportunities I've missed because of saying yes to things God hadn't called me to. Likewise, I wonder how much extra stress I put on my mental, emotional, and physical health by acting as if I would never run out of energy. None of us can strive to do it all without consequence.

Today I can be grateful that God's grace is sufficient even when I've been careless with my yeses. He promises restoration when I foolishly overcommit. Thank you, God, for that!

Prayer

Dear Heavenly Father, remind me that not every opportunity you offer should be a yes for me. Give me the wisdom to see what you've called me to and the courage to say no to those who may distract me from that path. Help me to stop trying to please people and, instead, be free to make wise commitments based on your priorities for my life.

Aging Gratefully in Action

Countless studies show that there is nothing more detrimental to our physical health than stress. Of course, there's no such thing as a life that is completely stress-free. But managing stress means employing wisdom as we make decisions as to what we can and can't do. Take a minute to ask God what you should focus on today, and then write down your top five priorities. I've found that focusing on the top five each day helps me assess how much time I actually have for any additional yeses.

Ladies Who Lunch

Finding Community in Midlife

Bear one another's burdens and, so fulfill the law of Christ.
GALATIANS 6:2 ESV

Laughter roared from a table in the back. Their matching red hats shouted that they were together on purpose. I was only in my twenties when I first observed them, but they left a lasting impression. I longed to know who they were. Each well over age fifty, they seemed to savor life over shared desserts. I sat in the same restaurant fixing my blouse and questioning whether my lunch date found me attractive, while these women had a sense of comfort with themselves I'd never known.

Their freedom didn't come from getting their bodies just as they wanted or from checking off all the boxes on life's to-do lists. Instead, the joy they radiated was a by-product of something more genuine than worldly perfection or accomplishments. Theirs was a state of delight that comes from being in community. Togetherness holds a beauty that solo acts can never achieve. It is only when we are with and accepted by others that we feel safe to be fully ourselves.

Yet as we walk through midlife, community can feel daunting, especially if we've stepped out of it for a season. But community isn't optional for believers who want to live out God's purpose for their lives. We're not designed to do life alone. If the church is the body of Christ, living apart from community is like living without all the anatomical parts you need to function. As Scripture suggests in 1 Corinthians 12, whether you are an eye, ear, kidney, or big toe, you're not going to make it very long on your own. We need each other. We need to be part of a church body.

> **Togetherness holds a beauty that solo acts can never achieve.**

Biblically, community is also essential to finding joy in our walk of faith. The first church modeled a type of togetherness that most (in the United States at least) rarely experience. They were united on missions, sharing scrolls and sourdough, and worshiping the Lord together through teaching, fellowship, and prayer (Acts 2:42–47). This lifestyle led to others being saved. Their joy was full as they served God together.

But don't misunderstand. This type of joy comes not by showing up but by opening up. If you can make it through church without seeing anyone who knows your name, you haven't found community there. Community only happens when we surrender to the process of getting to know others and being known.

This may feel difficult at first. I worry that midlife has stolen my resilience. I've grown even more sensitive to rejection. The lure of "you're just fine on your own" appeals to my fragile ego. Inside I whine, *Do I have to put the effort in and get to know people? That's hard!*

God's answer is yes. The awkwardness of entering a new community becomes obviously worth it when, months or years later, you feel like you've found your people.

The instruction in Galatians 6:2 (ESV) to "bear one another's burdens" is a beautiful thing to behold in community. Something miraculous happens when you find a group of people who care for your needs, pray for you, support you, and allow you to do the same for them. You lose the weight of carrying the heavy load of life alone. And others do the same. I guess you could say this is God's perfect weight-loss plan!

But if we don't engage in community in midlife, the consequences can be harmful. Shouldering life alone increases the burden on our aging bodies and souls. If we don't put effort into finding community at this stage of life, we may find ourselves isolated and alone when we enter the next.

Studies show that trying to do life outside community is common and dangerous. One-third of adults ages forty-five or older feel lonely, while one fourth of adults ages sixty-five and older are considered to be socially isolated. Social isolation is as likely a contributor to premature death as smoking and is associated with a 29 percent greater risk of heart disease and a 32 percent greater risk of stroke. Plus, those who are alone later in life have higher rates of depression and anxiety and a 68 percent greater risk of hospitalization.[11] When God instructs us to be in community, He does so because He knows it's good for us. We need each other in order to be healthier . . . in every way.

Sure, community can also be challenging. I understand if you've been hurt by people or past situations within community. I have too, my friend. It's painful. Yet isolation is not the way to heal. Instead we must grieve the loss. Take a deep breath. Pray hard for courage, and start anew. Remember the adage: every friend you've ever had was once a stranger.

Today I can be grateful that God designed me to be part of a body and that He created me for community. I can be thankful this is the context in which He designed me to thrive. I don't have to bear the weight of this world alone; I can share it with others as we all learn to lean more on Jesus together.

Prayer

Dear Heavenly Father, thank you for creating us to be people who do best in community. Help me to find that community today. Where you've already placed me in healthy Christian community, thank you for this gift. Where I'm still needing a group to fit in with, please hear my request today and lead me to the community you have for me.

Aging Gratefully in Action

There's an unsurpassed beauty in the connection we experience through opening our homes to others. Hospitality doesn't require a Pinterest-worthy spread or perfect decor. We make others feel most welcome not when our baseboards are clean or our counters are spotless, but when we're willing to open our hearts and share our stories. Some store-bought treats, a fresh pot of coffee, and colorful paper plates are enough to make a guest feel special. Think of two or three women you could invite over, and don't be afraid to keep it simple. Add a conversation starter like, "What's one dream you still have for your life?" and watch how strangers create community over cookies and conversation.

Coming Out of Your Shell

The Blessings of New Friendships at Midlife

Two are better than one, because they have a good return for their labor: If either of them falls down, one can help the other up. But pity anyone who falls and has no one to help them up.

ECCLESIASTES 4:9–10

While loneliness has become an epidemic among young people, loneliness peaks at three key times during adult life: the late twenties, late eighties, and the mid-fifties, according to a recent study.[12]

I remember that season of solitude in my late twenties. It felt like everyone was sending "Save the Dates" while I was still hoping to get a date. Work was so busy that office friendships were the only ones I could maintain. Keeping the TV volume high helped me not feel so alone at home.

Likewise, I can only imagine how lonely the late eighties may feel. When those close to you have gone or are no longer mobile enough for outings or visits, life must feel quiet. Maybe that's why elderly friends and relatives I've visited also keep their televisions blaring.

But in midlife, when age changes everything, friendships can be hard to find. Pools of potential friends that centered around kids' activities or office mates were once easy to swim in. But at this stage of life, it may feel like the pool is closed for the season. Loneliness rubs like a blister from a new pair of shoes. You feel it coming on, but you hope you'll get used to it so the sting will go away.

Friendships spark our souls and steady our hearts. Those parts of our personalities we've been afraid to let show are affirmed as acquaintances morph into confidants. As Proverbs 27:9 declares, "The heartfelt counsel of a friend is as sweet as perfume and incense" (NLT).

Chances are you can think back and remember a time when God sent you a friend. Maybe it was your first week at a new school. Perhaps the girl who invited you to sit with her at lunch was your bestie until the eighth grade. Or maybe it was later in life. You were new to the office, but she stopped by your desk to see if you wanted in on the coffee run. It's that first move that's so daunting. We long for an inner circle but fear rejection. Riddling through our brains come all the reasons why someone wouldn't prefer to spend time with us. *I'm too loud . . . I'm too much . . . I'm too quiet . . .* But these are the lies we must silence if we're ever to unearth the treasure that friendship in midlife has to offer.

I confess. We moved a few years ago. Between the pandemic and the busyness of our family schedule, I realized that though I had a lot of names and numbers in my contacts, my list of close friends was too short. So I sent a text message inviting a woman I'd met at church to have coffee. It was totally awkward. But she said yes. And the process of getting to know a new friend began.

Researchers say it takes forty to sixty hours to have a casual friendship, eighty to one hundred hours together to be classified as a real friend, and more than two hundred hours together to become good friends.[13] If this is true, we can count on those first three, four, or five lunches or coffee meetups to feel forced. Making friends requires intentionality. It's just like my mom always said—if you want to have friends, you have to be a friend. You work to find what you have in common and start building on that foundation.

Midlife is not the time for us to become turtles. Turtles are solitary creatures, uniquely designed to do life alone. Outside of short seasons of mating, courtship, and nesting, you'll rarely see them together. They don't like to be touched, rarely vocalize, and prefer not to have other turtles around.

The older I get, there are days when I feel turtle-like. Then I look in the mirror and realize I have no shell. We were made for friendship. God modeled this back in Genesis when He created Adam. He said it wasn't good for man to be alone, so He created Eve too (Genesis 2:18). Isolation contradicts our very composition. That's likely why Scripture recognizes and lauds the title of friend. Abraham was called a friend of God in Isaiah 41:8, while Exodus 33:11 tells us that Moses spoke with God as a man speaks to a friend.

While it's tempting as we age to grow cozier inside our own habits and homes, we can't emotionally afford to retreat. Instead, this is a prime time to build relationships with those whom we know will strengthen, encourage, and walk with us through the next season or seasons of life. I once heard it said that if you're looking for friends to sharpen you, don't hang out with butter knives. What a clever reminder to invest in the friendships that grow us and avoid those who leave us feeling dull.

In John 15:13–15, we read that Jesus demonstrated the greatest act of friendship by laying down His life for us. Then we're encouraged by the truth that we're all God's friends if we do what He commands. If Jesus is the friend who "sticks closer than a brother" (Proverbs 18:24), then we know we always have a friend we can rely on, even when human friendships shift. The gospel message is one of pursuit, sacrifice, reconciliation, and commitment—what a fantastic model for friendship.

Today I can be grateful that I'm never too old to make new friends. God designed my human heart to enjoy interaction, and I can thank Him for the opportunity to come out of my shell and to feel rejuvenated and refreshed from the gift of friendship in midlife.

Prayer

Dear Heavenly Father, give me the courage to stay connected to friends through this season of midlife. If my list of close friends is short, help me to grow it. Show me where to find friends, and give me the courage to make it through the awkwardness of getting to know someone new. Help me to be a good friend who is not afraid to be intentional about accountability and growth.

Aging Gratefully in Action

Feeling low in the friendship department? Make a list of a few women you know with whom you would want to pursue a deeper friendship. Instead of feeling envious of those women who seem to go out to lunch with their friends all the time, make your own fun. Invite some prospective friends out to lunch or coffee. Remember, it takes time to make new friends, so don't give up after just one outing. Plan a second. Don't have anyone on that list? Pray and ask God to send you some new friends.

Marriage in Midlife

Changing and Growing Together

Above all, keep loving one another earnestly,
since love covers a multitude of sins.
1 PETER 4:8 ESV

The best you'll ever look is on your wedding day." I'm sure many have said it over the centuries, but its hopeless tone has always bothered me. The first day of marriage shouldn't be the climax. Day one can't be as good as it gets!

Popular marriage teacher Jimmy Evans offers a creative suggestion for making sure day one isn't the pinnacle. He proposes that it would be more accurate for the bride and groom to look their worst at the wedding. The bride should wear a hospital gown to symbolize the hurt she brings with her, hair custom-styled by her pillow. The groom could wear a ripped-up military uniform to reflect the battles of his past. Both should carry suitcases to represent the baggage they'd inevitably bring into the relationship.[14]

Of course, the beauty of a pristinely dressed woman in white joined to her handsomely attired husband gives us a picture of how Jesus and His church will be united someday. But I wonder if a banged-up bride and a flawed fellow aren't a more accurate description of how our marriages start.

Instead of looking at the framed wedding photo and lamenting, "That was the best we've ever been," what if we gained a fresh perspective on the beauty of marriage in midlife? Our bodies may be different than they once were. But the richness that comes with years or decades of building trust and mutual respect holds a beauty of its own.

My grandparents celebrated seventy-four years of marriage before their passing. My parents have celebrated fifty and counting. Perhaps we should be celebrating anniversaries with as much gusto as we put in to the wedding day. As anyone who has been married for more than a week knows, staying married is a lot more difficult than getting married.

You see, we enter our unions with passion, but as we age, unless that passion turns to compassion, we'll grow apart instead of together. Marriage offers a type of sanctification rivaled only by parenthood. It can form us into people who are more caring, understanding, and trusting if we let it. *Compassion* literally means "to suffer together." I've found that some of the most beautiful memories in almost twenty years of marriage are from those times when the hurts of life turned us toward each other.

> **Marriage offers a type of sanctification rivaled only by parenthood.**

Likewise, when we're exhausted from having the same argument for decades or when we feel the loneliness of being home alone, together, for the first time in years, 1 Peter 4:8 reminds us, "Above all, keep loving one another earnestly, since love covers a multitude of sins" (ESV). When we don't have the energy (or hormones) to bring back that loving feeling, we can remember that love is something we choose.

Marriage in midlife gives us new opportunities. If family schedules lighten, there may suddenly be more time for spending together. Of course, the temptation will be to slip into synchronized lives. You're doing the same things each day, but just not together. His History Channel plays in one room while her Hallmark plays in the other. It may take intentionality to recognize that being home at the same time doesn't count as a date night.

Becoming one flesh, as Jesus described in Matthew 19:4–6, isn't a process that's completed at a milestone anniversary. It's a daily surrender. It's constant submission to each other and the Lord (Ephesians 5:22–27). It's a seemingly unending exercise in forgiveness.

The strength of our bond at midlife sets the tone for what's ahead. In marriage, as in life, it's not how you start—it's how you finish. This applies not just as the anniversaries accumulate but to our attitudes each and every day. If our goal is to finish better than we start, we posture ourselves for long-term marriage success when we approach this as a goal for each day we're together.

Today I can be grateful that marriage in midlife gives me the opportunity to explore and experience greater depth in my marriage. I can grow in my love and compassion for my spouse so that my marriage can continue to flourish.

Prayer

Dear Heavenly Father, thank you for the blessing of marriage at midlife. Help me to continue to submit to the sanctification process that marriage brings. Show me how to be a spouse who loves well and who desires to finish even better than she started.

Aging Gratefully in Action

If you're married, when's the last time you thought about the accomplishment and beauty of the years you've had together? The Bible's promise for married people is that there will be struggle. So there's no shame or blame if you look back on your marriage and see more hard times than good. Thank God for His sustaining grace that has carried you through. Write down the traits you are most thankful for in your spouse. You'll be amazed to see how intentionally focusing on his best assets can reignite passion if that's faded over time.

Empty Nest, Full Heart

Fresh Grace for When the Flock Flies

. . . who satisfies you with good so that your
youth is renewed like the eagle's.
PSALM 103:5 ESV

There's something about the sight of a graduate's cap and gown that stirs deep emotion within me. I can hardly see senior prom pictures without crying. I'm acutely aware of how many years I have left before my entire flock flies away. The thought of being without them sounds lonely. Extremely lonely.

Maybe you're reading this today and you never had children. Perhaps that wasn't by choice. Or you've wrestled that empty-nest feeling for years. Maybe for you, those words sound like a prison sentence. You wonder just how vacant your home will feel when it's just you and the dog all day long.

It seems we have two ways of viewing our empty nests. One is like a hollow vacuum with the life sucked out of it. We can walk around the house as if someone's stolen our prized possessions and mourn their loss.

But there's a better way. As parents we're to train our children in the way they should go (Proverbs 22:6). "Go" may be the operative word in that sentence. We're to raise them to leave and cleave—to become responsible, God-loving, and God-fearing adults who can forage their own way through this world and establish their own households. This means that empty nests aren't hollow. They're healthy. They symbolize children who have grown and flown.

Yes, the vacancy is real. Yes, it feels strange to no longer run the dishwasher twice a day and have the couch pillows stay in the exact place you put them. But this isn't game over. It's mission accomplished. Congratulations! You've seen the fulfillment of a decades-long investment.

Of course, our purpose as parents doesn't end when we get laid off from our full-time parenting gigs. Those kids will likely still need our wisdom, recipes, money, and laundry facilities. There may be weddings to help plan and baby showers to host. Lonely late-night calls or texts will still need answering. While the temptation to keep parenting like you used to may feel ever ready to flare, this is yet another opportunity to practice surrendering control. We can trust God to speak in those situations where our opinions are no longer invited or welcomed.

As our children require fewer resources, this is also the season to revisit our purpose. What has God wired us for? What gifts has He given us within His body that we haven't used because we've been too busy with our families? Are there dreams that were put on pause two decades ago that God wants to reawaken in our lives?

An empty nest gives a warm space for God to incubate the next part of our stories. In Isaiah 43:19, God gives this message through His prophet to His people: "For I am about to do something new. See, I have already begun! Do you not see it? I will make a pathway through the wilderness. I will create rivers in the dry wasteland" (NLT).

Though parenting may have felt like a wilderness, those years were far from a wasteland. But if the empty-nest season feels dry, this Scripture may encourage your thirst for what's next.

He doesn't leave us empty. He's ready to fill—our cups, our plates, and any uncomfortable hollows of confusion we feel inside over what to do next. An empty nest doesn't mean our purpose has flown away—it means we're preparing to experience something fresh and new.

What happens if you get stuck lamenting the loss? What if it's too hard to move forward because the transition hits you hard? *Remember when they were so little? Remember the "good old days" when they needed me?* That wise man Solomon instructs in Ecclesiastes 7:10, "Say not, 'Why were the former days better than these?' For it is not from wisdom that you ask this" (ESV). It's not that Solomon wants us to burn the family photo books. Rather, his caution is that by romanticizing the past, we can get trapped there. Wisdom is moving forward and embracing our new season, not wasting time pining over the past.

If you're facing an empty nest (or have had one for years), can you believe that God has something new for you to do? Can you believe that there's as much life to be lived and purpose to be revealed in the days ahead as there was in the days behind? It may sound cliché, but I know it's true. God isn't finished with you yet. Remember, time doesn't slow down as we age. As quickly as that season of active parenting whizzed by, the next season will likely keep pace.

In Psalm 57:1–2, the psalmist cries, "Have mercy on me, O God, have mercy! I look to you for protection. I will hide beneath the shadow of your wings until the danger passes by. I cry out to God Most High, to God who will fulfill his purpose for me" (NLT). It's that last line I love the most. He will fulfill His purpose for me now, just as He's done in the past.

Yes, a great part of His purpose may have been raising those children. But perhaps it's time to press Play on what He has next.

Today I can be grateful that that my purpose didn't graduate and move out with my children. God has more for me to do. I can thank Him that He is in the business of doing a new thing and that He will infuse what's left of my time on this earth with new purpose and opportunities.

Prayer

Dear Heavenly Father, help me to seek out your purpose for this next season of my life. Remind me of the dreams I once had. Rekindle in me a passion for what you've created me to do. Lead me and guide me to what's next in this new season. Help me to use any newfound time surplus wisely and for your glory.

Aging Gratefully in Action

If your home feels emptier now, why not share it? Hospitality affords you the opportunity to get to know new people while doing something meaningful. Offer to host small groups for young moms who don't want the pressure of cleaning while caring for babies and toddlers. Offer your backyard for a youth group barbeque. Or invite young adults or elderly persons who would otherwise eat alone to have a seat at your dinner table. Even if you don't feel like you have the gift of hospitality, being hospitable can assuage the loneliness that can come when you transition to an empty nest.

"Grandma" Status

Promotions to Roles of Influence

Older women likewise are to be reverent in behavior,
not slanderers or slaves to much wine. They are to teach
what is good, and so train the young women to love
their husbands and children, to be self-controlled, pure,
working at home, kind, and submissive to their own
husbands, that the word of God may not be reviled.
TITUS 2:3–5 ESV

Many years ago postpartum depression rendered me lost and confused. I'd always wanted to have children. Yet I felt overwhelmed and underwhelmed at the same time. *Was I doing it wrong? Was I messing up my children? Was I failing at motherhood because I wasn't enjoying it?*

The sign in the ladies' bathroom at church said, "Connect with a Titus 2 Mentor." I sent an email to the address posted on the stall and awaited my connection. The response came from a woman nearing eighty. She asked if we could meet at a local café. Her treat. It's astonishing how life-giving the offer of a free lunch out can be to a new mom.

Loretta had perfectly coifed silver hair. She had a southern gentleness to her style. We talked about her children, grand-children, and great-grandchildren. She graciously reminded me that though my stage of life felt difficult and unending, there would be a time when the nonstop sippy-cup refills and diaper changes would end. Loretta encouraged me to lean on the Lord on the days when I didn't feel I had the strength to be the kind of mom I wanted to be. Soon I realized I hadn't just gained a new friend—I'd gained a new grandma.

For some of us, even thinking about the "g" word—grandma—feels strange. I had a late start, so I'll still be parenting kids at home for a few more years. But for you, the promotion to grandma may have already come or is on the way.

But even if you're not a grandma and never plan to be, you are promoted to a role of influence as you age. The Bible is clear about this opportunity for women. God designed His family to work best when the older women are active in the discipleship of the younger. But we can choose whether or not to enter into this divine opportunity to be an influencer.

Influencer may be one of the most overused and underdefined words in our culture today. To be an influencer—according to these standards—you need gorgeous photographs on Instagram or clever videos on YouTube. But to truly influence someone's life—to make a difference—requires more than just showing them an image of what they could be. Image shouts, *Look at me.* Influence shouts, *I see you, and I'm here to help.*

Though we may feel like our influence is gone once we have wrinkles and gray hair, nothing could be further from the truth. The Bible teaches that this is when our influence counts. We're not out of the influencer business when we retire from jobs or child-rearing. We're just graduating into it. After retiring from roles we strived for years to attain, what if our greatest roles lie ahead of us?

In Titus 2:3–5, we are instructed:

> Similarly, teach the older women to live in a way that honors God. They must not slander others or be heavy drinkers. Instead, they should teach others what is good. These older women must train the younger women to love their husbands and their children, to live wisely and be pure, to work in their homes, to do good, and to be submissive to their husbands. Then they will not bring shame on the word of God. (NLT)

How do we accomplish this grand task list? We do it through both instruction and infusion.

Instruction is the way we teach and show other women how to navigate young life—from marriage to parenting to surviving the toddler stage. When we instruct, we have a voice that speaks into the lives of others. We encourage and guide them at whatever stage they're in.

But we also carry out the Titus 2 tasks through infusion. Have you ever enjoyed a cold glass of water infused with strawberries or raspberries? I love how the flavor has just a touch of fruity goodness. I don't think I'd like a glass of cucumber juice. But that hint of freshness elevates the flavor of the water. It gives it new dimension.

Likewise, the way our lives infuse the lives of the women who follow us is multilayered. We may have even greater influence by what we model for others than what we teach. Though some find teaching difficult, modeling reminds us that our whole lives are a witness—either to our testimony in Christ or to the stories we believe about ourselves.

For me, that story was the one I believed about my body and

my worth. Thinking back to elementary school, I don't recall a time when I ever truly felt comfortable with my body size. The journey through disordered eating and body dysmorphia has been a long one. But now I can see how God can use my story to help the next generation of women struggling with these same issues.

It's easy for me to teach this subject, but modeling requires me to fight the flesh daily. When I'm tempted to get caught up in the beauty rat race and fixate on my weight or appearance, I am reminded of who is watching. If I can't model being comfortable in my own skin, how can I possibly encourage others so that they can feel like they're unconditionally accepted and loved, no matter what they look like? Modeling is what makes us believable. Our showing can have a greater impact than our telling.

Plus, grandmas have privileges that moms don't. As mentors to the next generation of women, we may be able to see and speak into things that family members—those too close to the situation—can't call out or acknowledge. It often takes someone outside our cocoon to help us see where our wings are stuck.

One young mom was constantly frustrated by her child's clingy and whiny tendencies later in the day. She'd tried discipline, bribery, television, and everything else she could think of to create space to prepare dinner. Her mom recommended setting aside thirty minutes, much earlier in the day, to focus only on that child. She tried it and soon, the meal-time cling disappeared. Grandma discerned that the deeper issue couldn't be strategized away; she saw through to the real need that an exhausted mom couldn't.

Recent studies have shown that grandparents who help provide some care for grandchildren stay young longer.[15] Caring for children requires more energy and focus than caring for oneself. It keeps bodies active and minds sharp. But I also wonder if those who care for the next generation have a revitalized sense of purpose.

To this end, we can start acting like the biblical kind of "grandma" long before we have—or even if we never have—biological grandkids to spoil. We can apply the Titus 2 principles to how we live throughout midlife.

I'm not aging out of relevance—I'm aging into it.

Today I can be grateful that, biblically, my influencer status elevates at midlife. I'm not aging out of relevance—I'm aging into it.

Prayer

Dear Heavenly Father, thank you for the role you give me in midlife as an influencer. Whether it be to grandchildren, mentees, or younger women in my sphere of influence, thank you for the opportunity to redeem my own story by sharing it and modeling it to the generations that follow. Help me to lead others to a closer relationship with you.

Aging Gratefully in Action

Could God be calling you to mentor to a younger woman? Is there a woman in your life who needs your encouragement, help, or guidance? What would it look like to step into this heavenly calling and walk alongside her? Investments like these yield a far better return than any antiaging treatment. In other words, hanging out with younger women keeps you young. Try it and see how energizing it feels.

Cleaning Out the Junk Drawers

Putting the Past to Rest

Remember not the former things, nor consider the
things of old. Behold, I am doing a new thing, now
it springs forth, do you not perceive it? I will make
a way in the wilderness and rivers in the desert.
ISAIAH 43:18–19 ESV

We remodeled our kitchen last year and went without one for almost six months. I never realized how much I relied on this item. I'm not talking about the sink, dishwasher, or stove. Yes, life without these was a major inconvenience. But there was something strange that I found myself missing during that renovation: my junk drawer.

Where do you stash that receipt you may need later? Where do you put that random screw that must go to something but needs a home until you identify where? Random lids, twist ties, and pens, lots of pens . . . Where do they go without a junk drawer?

And cleaning out the junk drawer? That's actually a better test of personality than any psychological assessment. Do you throw it all away without consideration? Do you keep everything there just in case? Do you lift and assess every item and make carefully calculated decisions as to what stays and what goes?

There's no right way to clean out a junk drawer. But unless you do, you'll end up overflowing into a second junk drawer.

As we age, how many of us keep a junk drawer of memories? Maybe there are some regrets, some disappointments, or some hurts that we just can't pick up and process, so we leave them there, untouched.

But when aging coaxes us into cleaning out our mental junk drawers, we face a dilemma. We can either stare at the memories, pain, hurt, and regret and sort through them, or we become weighed down by the volume of overflow junk in our hearts.

Scripture gives us telling instructions on how to deal with the past. We're directed not to dwell on it. To forget it, even. Yet this can't mean taking memories, stuffing them in that drawer, and shutting it tight. We may convince ourselves that we've forgotten. But emotionally we carry that junk drawer with us, often not recognizing when bits of it spill into our relationships.

So how do we process our past? I've heard it said that, in Christ, we forgive and remember.[16] We lift that unidentified trinket from our heart's junk drawer. Then we ask God to help us identify it. Where did it come from? Why is it still there? Then, finally, we put it where it belongs. Sometimes that means simply laying it at the feet of Jesus.

Perhaps it's emotional garbage that needs to be examined for lies and then thrown in the fire. Or maybe it's past wounds that were never properly treated. We invite our Jehovah-Rapha—God, our healer—to come in like a skilled surgeon and push aside the scar tissue so our hurts can truly heal. We may also need to invite other professionals—Christian counselors, therapists, or friends—to help us mend.

Yes, Scripture does teach us not to stay stuck in our own histories. Isaiah 43:18–19 reads, "Forget the former things; do not dwell on the past. See, I am doing a new thing! Now it springs up; do you not perceive it? I am making a way in the wilderness and streams in the wasteland."

Likewise, Philippians 3:13–14 reminds us, "But I focus on this one thing: Forgetting the past and looking forward to what lies ahead, I press on to reach the end of the race and receive the heavenly prize for which God, through Christ Jesus, is calling us" (NLT).

Following these instructions authentically requires us to empty that junk drawer, to recognize that our God is just, kind, and big enough to help us face our emotional mess no matter how monstrous it feels. He can help us heal.

You see, healing is more about remembering than forgetting.[17] The most soothing balm to our hurts is the ability to see what Jesus did for us on the cross. Clearly seeing my own sin and what Jesus did to cover it is the secret to effectively sorting the trash from the treasure in our emotional junk drawers. Psalm 103:2–4 reminds us of this principle. "Bless the LORD, O my soul, and forget not all his benefits, who forgives all your iniquity, who heals all your diseases, who redeems your life from the pit, who crowns you with steadfast love and mercy" (ESV).

> The most soothing balm to our hurts is the ability to see what Jesus did for us on the cross.

Today I can be grateful that the cross of Jesus allows me to remember and heal. I can rest knowing that God's grace is enough to cover all of my own guilt and shame as well as the hurts I bear from wrongs committed against me. As I walk through midlife, He alone can give me the courage to sort through my past while remembering who holds my future.

Prayer

Dear Heavenly Father, thank you for the gift of healing. Thank you that you are willing to walk with me as I examine my own heart. Help me to pull out the emotional junk that I've carried, and sort it rightly according to your truth.

Aging Gratefully in Action

There's nothing more beautiful than a person at peace. If your emotional junk drawer feels like it's overflowing, now is the time to find someone trustworthy and biblically sound to help you sort it out. Don't wait. There's no shame in getting help—the only shame is in living a life weighed down by emotional baggage.

Freedom of Forgiveness

Embracing God's Grace for Mistakes

> Get rid of all bitterness, rage, anger, harsh words, and
> slander, as well as all types of evil behavior. Instead,
> be kind to each other, tenderhearted, forgiving one
> another, just as God through Christ has forgiven you.
> EPHESIANS 4:31–32 NLT

I recently met a woman who told me she was saving money for counseling for her children, not college. "I think they'll need therapy more than a thesis," she joked.

I laughed at her honesty. Our children have no choice but to be raised by imperfect parents. Likewise, our spouses have only one option—an imperfect mate. Our friends, bosses, neighbors, and extended families may desire perfection from us, but they won't get it.

For a recovering perfectionist, that's a jagged little pill. *There's no way I can be perfect? Trying harder won't ever render me faultless and flawless?*

So what do we do when we find ourselves wallowing in our own imperfections, sorrowfully navel-gazing over our own short-comings? It's only when we recognize that perfection apart from Christ is unattainable that we can fully embrace grace.

Grace is a concept that I'd heard about in songs at church. I knew it had to do with Jesus and His sacrifice on the cross. But the meaning felt fuzzy. Was grace about thanking God for food or getting to heaven?

Today I understand grace differently. Grace is free and unde-served favor. Grace is extending love and kindness when pun-ishment and pain are deserved. A deeper understanding of grace is key to our maturity as healthy individuals and as followers of Jesus, growing in Christlikeness. As we reach midlife, we have a grand opportunity to experience God's grace for our past so that we can flourish in our future. But this requires forgive-ness—forgiving others as we embrace the ways we have been divinely forgiven.

The only way through our litany of past mistakes is to con-fess our sins and know God is faithful and just to forgive us of them (1 John 1:9). Perhaps this is why German theologian Martin Luther said, "the entire life of believers is to be one of repentance."[18] There isn't one day that I've lived perfectly. Thus, the only solution for all of my imperfections is to keep the posi-tion of my heart contrite.

I haven't been a perfect parent. I haven't been a perfect spouse. Don't ask how many times I've failed as a daughter, sister, em-ployee, or friend. I didn't do any of it perfectly, but that's okay. That's why Jesus came. If I could have done it perfectly, I wouldn't have needed Him.

Jesus teaches us to take the forgiveness He grants and then extend it to others who've wronged us. In Matthew 18:21–22, Peter asks Jesus how many times he has to forgive someone who sins against him. Peter offers seven times as a generous amount.

But Jesus replies, "No, not seven times . . . but seventy times seven" (NLT). When hurt or offended, even after the 490th time, we're still to forgive.

What about when we find ourselves making the same mistake for time five hundred? How do we find the courage to pick up, move on, and try again?

Some say you have to forgive yourself, but I don't find any place in Scripture where that's instructed. I must be more grieved by how my sin hurt the heart of God than I am obsessed over how I fell short of my own standards. I wonder if we get stuck wallowing in the sins of our past because of this popularized concept of self-forgiveness.

> **I must be more grieved by how my sin hurt the heart of God than I am obsessed over how I fell short of my own standards.**

Instead of focusing on my trying to forgive and free myself, I must believe that only Jesus truly has the power to release me. It's not that I'm a prisoner locked in my own cage, sitting inside the cell with the key. It's that God is the warden, and because of what Jesus did on the cross, He's swung my cell door open. My only choice is whether or not I walk out.

In Psalm 65:3, we read, "Though we are overwhelmed by our sins, you forgive them all" (NLT). The solution is not accepting our own forgiveness but believing in God's unrelenting grace.

Only then, by operating in the power of the miraculous work done for us, do we have the ability to see others' sins and forgive them. We can learn from the parable of the unmerciful servant, found in Matthew 18, that when we recognize the lavish amount of forgiveness poured onto us through the grace of Jesus, we can splash some onto others.

Today I can be grateful that forgiveness isn't up to me. I can thank God for the free gift of His grace and that He loved me enough to pick me up out of my imperfection and offer Jesus's blameless life as the pardon for all of my mistakes.

Prayer

Dear Heavenly Father, teach me to forgive as you have forgiven me. Help me to let go of offenses I've clung to. Show me how to release others from the pain they have caused me and how to trust you for justice. And most of all, help me to walk in the truth that because you have completely forgiven me, I can freely offer forgiveness to others.

Aging Gratefully in Action

Forgiveness lifts a heavy spirit. You'll be surprised at how much lighter you'll feel after releasing grudges that bog you down spiritually, mentally, and physically. Accept the gift of God's forgiveness, then ask Him to show you who or what you need to forgive. Consider writing a list of the offenses you dwell on most, and pray over them daily. As you pray, ask God to show you where you are withholding forgiveness.

Sandwiched

Caring for Children and Parents

Cast your burden on the Lord, and he will sustain you;
he will never permit the righteous to be moved.
Psalm 55:22 esv

We are T-minus seven days away from a family vacation, which means packing for five (at least my husband packs himself) and remembering to throw away the old potatoes (lest we face that dead-animal smell upon our return). It also means stopping the mail, sorting through kids' summer clothes to find swimsuits, and buying dog treats to make the pet sitter's job easier. Tomorrow I'm hosting a seventy-fifth birthday party for my mother-in-law and twenty of her friends. I should probably clean and prepare refreshments for that. Oh, and I'm not exaggerating when I say I have twenty-three different places to be in the days before we leave. Plus, I need to finish this manuscript.

But Mom called a few minutes ago and said my dad will

be having open-heart surgery. I should be there. So instead of doing all these things in seven days, I'll now do them in three. Pardon me while I head into a phone booth and twirl into my Wonder Woman costume. *If only.*

"Sandwich generation" is the term tossed around to describe what it feels like to have kids at home who need you and aging parents who also require attention. Yet I wonder if the sandwich imagery isn't a little too nice. I need to care for my parents. I need to care for my children. I also need to care for myself, my career, my marriage . . . Instead of feeling competent, I'm overcome with all this neediness. I'm not the deli turkey in between two slices of honey wheat. That sounds nice and cozy.

No. I'm not sandwiched. I'm stretched. It feels like I'm strapped to the silly torture machine from the movie *The Princess Bride*. With all sides pulling at once, I should be as flexible as a gymnast after all this stretching.

Walking through the declining health of parents while growing children at home is no easy feat. I can't just skip town and leave directions for the kids to be watered every other day. But as I age, I feel the stress and strain of the compounding details. I once feared that my brain was dulling. Now I wonder if I'm simply asking more of it. From remembering the dog's medication, to camp applications, to which uniform is for away games, to googling "what is a nephrologist," I feel like I need a personal secretary. The Queen had one. Perhaps there's something to that.

Even if I had administrative support for my personal life, I still don't have enough within me to take care of it all. The list is too long. There's too much I *could* worry about. Wonder Woman's bracelets couldn't deflect the bullets of all the stress shooting in my direction.

Instead of a superhero costume or a secretary, what I need is more grace. God's grace offers shelter for me through every trial while sanctifying me on my journey toward Christlikeness. His grace sustains me daily. Make that hourly. No, it's every minute.

Something that sustains our strength is called sustenance. It's a word we commonly use in reference to food or nourishment. But in high-stress seasons in which we are caretakers on overload, sustenance is exactly what we crave. I cannot sustain myself. I cannot bear alone the pressure of kids' college applications, career commitments, and decisions about parents' medical treatment.

Remember Isaiah 46:4? "Even to your old age I am he, and to gray hairs I will carry you. I have made, and I will bear; I will carry and will save" (ESV).

He will carry. He will save. That's a promise I cling to during times of crisis. I picture myself hobbling along, schlepping a heavy bag of to-do lists and burdens. Then Jesus grabs my crutches, swoops me up like I'm weightless, and carries me up the hills of my struggle.

Psalm 73:26 also speaks into my need for sustenance. It reads, "My flesh and my heart may fail, but God is the strength of my heart and my portion forever." Though on my own, I'd run out of energy and strength, He offers me an ample portion of sustaining grace.

I don't have to worry about being enough for all the people and all the things. He is enough. As Psalm 28:7 reminds us, "The LORD is my strength and my shield; in him my heart trusts, and I am helped; my heart exults, and with my song I give thanks to him" (ESV).

Today I can be grateful that God promises to carry me when I'm overwhelmed. God's grace sustains me when I'm pulled to the breaking point. Though it feels like it's all on me, I know I can rest in His grace. He's the only one who really has it all under control.

Prayer

Dear Heavenly Father, thank you for sustaining me even in the midst of feeling pulled in a dozen directions. Thank you that even when I'm on the brink, you won't let me break.

Aging Gratefully in Action

The stress of caring for parents and children simultaneously can take us to some unhealthy places physically, emotionally, and mentally. What kind of stress-management techniques do you rely on? Do you have a go-to way to de-stress? Plan these into your regular life, but don't neglect them when caretaking responsibilities escalate. Even if you can't fit into your schedule a full twenty-minute walk, just take five. Likewise, if an hour nap isn't possible, try lying down for fifteen. Have a stress-relief playlist ready on your phone filled with songs that help you rest, relax, and worship. Lifting a song of thanks to Him (perhaps while taking a relaxing bath) can take the stress off like nothing else.

Recipe for Rest

True Rest Is Rooted in Trust

Truly my soul finds rest in God; my salvation comes
from him. Truly he is my rock and my salvation;
he is my fortress, I will never be shaken.
Psalm 62:1–2

Why do women go on diets? I bet you're thinking of the obvious answers like weight loss or changing body size or shape. But I have a secret that may blow your mind. After coaching and talking to women who struggle with body image issues for almost a decade, I've learned that what women want most is to stop the struggle. The reason why we go on diets is so we can rest.

Of course, there's no rest at the beginning of the diet. Not even close. There's a lot of planning and striving—it takes focus. It takes work. It takes discipline and determination. But the greatest hope of a woman starting a new diet is not just that she will get the body of her dreams. It's that at the end of six weeks or six months, she'll no longer have to diet anymore. She'll be free from worrying about food or obsessing over her size.

Dieters are rest seekers, dreaming of a day when we can just be normal with food and not have to diet anymore. And that day, that rest seems to only come legally if we can earn it. Even if you've never been on a diet in your life, there's likely something similar you've done with the secret goal of being able to rest when it was finished. Whether it's cleaning the house or pushing through a big project at work, there are numerous ways we work to earn our reprieve. Culture tells us we deserve rest only when we work for it.

But that's not God's recipe for rest. Scripture tells us that Jesus alone offers us true rest. There's no formula for being good enough or doing enough to deserve it. Instead, it's a part of our inheritance as God's adopted children. His yoke is easy. His burden is light. That same passage in Matthew 11:28 reminds us that if we come to Him, He gives us rest. There's no mention of working for it.

Why do we struggle with rest in midlife? Among other reasons, it's our striving that muddies the matter. We build false identities on accomplishments we think will satisfy. We set up deadlines and goals to try to win imaginary contests where the ultimate prize is joy. *If I can just get this done, then I'll feel good.* We promise ourselves it will be enough, but it never is.

Yet whatever we can't rest from, we become slaves to. In Deuteronomy 5:15, God reminds the Israelites that rest is a privilege of their freedom. "Remember that you were once slaves in Egypt, but the Lord your God brought you out with his strong hand and powerful arm. That is why the Lord your God has commanded you to rest on the Sabbath day" (NLT).

The Sabbath is important not just because God commands it. Our ability to sabbath—or not sabbath—offers important insight for us to see what's holding us captive. If we can't take a pause one designated day each week, we're forced to ask hard questions about our schedules. *Am I in charge of my calendar, or does it rule me? Am I working because I get to or because I have to?* When we're so controlled, so dominated, and so pressured that we can't take a rest, we've become slaves to whatever rules us.

If you're like me, you may struggle to believe you'll be okay if you press Pause on the busyness. Productivity is next to godliness. Culture screams, "Your goals won't wait for you to take a break!" Our default mode is to prove we're worthy.

I recently read an interesting study about women who've been through trauma. One commonality is how we have a difficult time resting.[19] This resonated. Years ago I didn't want my husband to know I was napping every day. Sure, I had young kids and an autoimmune thyroid issue—but I didn't want him to think I was lazy. When I finally told him about the guilt and shame I'd felt over my daily nap time, he was shocked. It didn't bother him at all.

What is the recipe for rest? The secret sauce is building our trust in Jesus. Only then can we recognize how we'll never accomplish enough on this earth to feel like we've earned a break. When plans to rest get swallowed by the "just a little bit more" monster, we have to turn up our trust before we can back away.

An inability to rest can also reveal ways we're caught in the trap of trying to build our own kingdoms. Are we overworking because we long to be seen, noticed, promoted, or praised? Are we striving to advance like our neighbors or friends, or are we trying to be more like Jesus?

The kind of rest Jesus demonstrated wasn't about religious laws or rules. In fact, by healing a man on the Sabbath (John 5), Jesus showed the Pharisees their rules were more about earning a place in heaven than resting in grace. Rules beam us right back to striving. We believe we *can* work hard enough to earn our place with God.

But the message of the gospel is distinct. In fact, Christianity is the only religion on the planet where the work is already done for us.[20] In other words, as Christ-followers, we should be the best at rest. If God can take care of my sin problem, there's nothing in my life He can't handle. This kind of rest is productive toward our ultimate goals—knowing God and living for His purpose and His kingdom.

True rest comes when we realize the earthly assets we chase will never bring us the rest they promise. The recipe for rest is only found in Jesus.

Today I can be grateful that God provided a way for me to rest through Jesus. When the pressures of midlife leave me weary, tired, burdened, and spent, my way of escape is not to work harder in a vain attempt to get it all done and earn rest. Instead, I can retreat to the Father. Through spending time alone with Him, I can find refreshment, restoration, and true rest.

Prayer

*Dear Heavenly Father, thank you for your offer of rest.
Thank you that Jesus did all the work to free me from
the slavery of sin so that now I can rest in Him.*

Aging Gratefully in Action

Exhaustion doesn't benefit anyone—physically, mentally, or spiritually. What kind of rest is missing in your life? Do you have time to yourself or dedicated time to simply breathe and be? If regular rest feels absent from your life, consider scheduling intentional blocks of downtime. Sometimes even a twenty-minute nap during the day can yield better sleep at night, helping you feel more rested the next day. Similarly, setting aside one day a week for a sabbath rest is a biblical idea that does the heart, mind, and body good. Taking this time to be intentional about connecting with God and disconnecting with worry, work, and distractions can restore a sense of peace. Spend some time today asking God if you need to add more rest to your routine.

Saying Goodbye

Holding on to Faith in the Season of Goodbyes

Fear not, for I am with you; be not dismayed, for I
am your God; I will strengthen you, I will help you,
I will uphold you with my righteous right hand.
ISAIAH 41:10 ESV

Melancholy. That's the word I'd use to describe my
paternal grandfather. Trauma he'd experienced in
the South Pacific during World War II likely added
to the depth of his moods. At the end of every visit, Grandpa
would say, "Well, this is probably the last time you'll see me
here. I'm headed to heaven soon."

For more than a decade, my grandpa left me with those
words. By the time I reached my teen years, I found it plain
annoying. Why did he always talk about dying? Why did he
always drop the "this is the last time" bomb on us as we left?

But now I wonder if he had the courage to say what most
would rather not. Perhaps the way he reminded us that this

"could be the last time . . ." wasn't an assault but a gift. My grandparents lived far away, in Arkansas. We only saw them once a year. Acknowledging the possibility that I may not see him again gave me the opportunity to hug a little tighter and process what each goodbye really meant.

The word *goodbye* is a shortened form of the expression "God be with ye." Sometime in the late 1500s, the greeting was condensed into just one word.[21] Even the French word for *goodbye* is a beautiful sentiment of sending someone into God's arms. The word *adieu* comes from the root words *a*, meaning "to," and *Dieu*, meaning "God," proclaiming a send-off to God's care (with an extra touch of French flair).

The apostle Paul ends his letters with phrases like, "The grace of the Lord Jesus be with you," "Grace with you," and "Grace to you." He reminds his readers of God's grace with each goodbye. I believe that's intentional. He's not just leaving them—he's placing them in God's care.

Midlife is when we may begin to recognize our own mortality. Though senior-citizen status once felt forever away, we now get mail from AARP and wonder how it could possibly be addressed to us. Coming to grips with our limited number of days is one thing, but midlife also often means walking through friends and family members, especially those from older generations, making their exits to eternity.

At age twenty-five I flew back to Arkansas to attend grandpa's funeral. And though I'd not been to visit in several years, I didn't have regrets. I knew we'd made peace with our parting.

I contrast that with another goodbye we faced a few years ago. Our family walked through a six-month stage-four cancer journey with my father-in-law. As I stood at his bedside the day before he passed, I felt a different sort of heaviness with that *adieu*. When goodbyes surprise us, they can feel overwhelming.

There's no trick to handling loss. I can't write you a list of five ways to make grieving easier. But at this stage in life, I'm planning more funerals than baby showers. I believe the only path is through the grief, not around it. We feel both the heaviness of loss and the fragility of life.

I read an article by Paul Tripp on aging in which he said that one of the main reasons we struggle with getting older is because we were never meant to die.[22] Somewhere, deep within our souls, we know that we weren't created for death to be our destiny. Though as Christ-followers we have eternity ahead of us to spend with Jesus, we may still struggle to make sense of loss, especially when it feels like it has come too soon.

Isaiah 41:10 reads, "Fear not, for I am with you; be not dismayed, for I am your God; I will strengthen you, I will help you, I will uphold you with my righteous right hand" (ESV). When the time for goodbye comes, it's comforting to know we are not alone. I dwell on the words "be not dismayed" from this instruction. Even when the parting is unexpected, God is still in control. He's not letting anyone go from His care. Not the one we lost, and not us.

And because He helps us through our grief, we are equipped to help those around us as they say goodbye too. In 2 Corinthians 1:3–4, Paul says, "God is our merciful Father and the source of all comfort. He comforts us in all our troubles so that we can comfort others. When they are troubled, we will be able to give them the same comfort God has given us" (NLT).

Today I can be grateful that I can feel the peace of my Savior no matter how difficult the goodbye. I know I can lean on His grace to be enough as I process the loss of the ones sent into His care.

Prayer

Dear Heavenly Father, give us peace through our seasons of goodbyes. Grant us the grace we need to keep trusting and relying on you for the hope and the future that you promise. Even in our grief, remind us of your faithfulness.

Aging Gratefully in Action

Our goodbyes can always be beautiful when we live a life without regret. A counselor once told me to keep short accounts with God, quickly repenting when we know we've sinned against Him. This is good advice for all our relationships, according to Matthew 5:23–24. Even when we've been careless with our words, angry or frustrated, and mistreated someone close to us, there's always an opportunity to make things right. Until there's not. Making confession, repentance, and forgiveness a regular practice can keep our relationships healthy as we age and prepare to one day say goodbye.

All Those Candles

How Age Helps You Burn Bright for God's Kingdom

Set your minds on things that are above,
not on things that are on earth.
COLOSSIANS 3:2

Would you go back to being thirty? I can answer without hesitation. No, never. I have no desire to go back to that age again.

Apparently I'm not alone. Dr. Jay Olshansky, an epidemiologist, researches ways to slow down aging. In his role as a professor at UIC School of Public Health in Chicago, he asks his students a question: If you could stop biological aging, at what age would you make it?[23]

Twentysomethings respond as though thirty is ancient. But when Dr. Olshansky asked his ninety-five-year-old father about his best year, his response was swift: fifty.

According to a 2013 Harris Poll, fifty is when stress starts to diminish for many.[24] Other studies call this "the Happiness U."

Happiness peaks around age twenty, dips until age forty, and then gradually rises again. By fifty you're solidly on the upswing. In fact, age seventy is when psychological well-being and life satisfaction peak for many, according to Arthur Stone, a professor at the University of Southern California and author of a 2015 study on this topic.[25]

But it's not just that we're happier because the biggest stressors of life fade. I wonder if we're not also happier because we've finally learned that we're not in charge. Perhaps, as we age, we have the opportunity to gradually understand what Solomon said about the shortness and vanity of life.

Vanity may conjure images of someone addicted to their mirror. But that's not the entire definition. Vanity means anything that won't last—something fleeting. That's our life here on this earth.

Recognizing that life expires can be a powerful motivator to focus on what lasts and turn away from the frivolous pursuits that occupy too much of our time. When I get to heaven, I want Jesus to see what I did for His kingdom, not how great I was at keeping wrinkles at bay. However many decades I have left here, I hope to use them to burn bright for Him.

I remember as a teenager going to youth camp and singing songs asking God to "light a fire" inside of me. He was faithful. I'd leave those weeks with explosive energy, ready to tell the world about what Jesus has done. But it's easy now to get caught up in the pull of this life. There are so many distractions and demands. The urgent shoves away the important.

Recently I watched a documentary on the revival happening in Iran. One of the missionary women interviewed had the opportunity to return home to California for a sabbatical. When they asked her if she was glad to be back and relieved to be out of the dangerous war zone where hiding from Al Qaeda was a daily chore, her response was no, that there are too many things here to distract her from serving Jesus.[26] I gasped! Her view of what matters in this life had changed completely. I long for that. Do you?

So how do we keep our fire for Jesus burning bright? Now is perhaps the best time in our lives to live like it's true—to live as if we believe that this world is not the one that matters. Live as if it's our souls that will someday go on, not our bodies. This means caring for the spiritual condition of our hearts with greater vigor than we care for the physical condition.

What is the equivalent of heart-healthy Cheerios for your soul? The secret may be found in Colossians 3:2: "Set your minds on things that are above, not on things that are on earth" (ESV). We may worry about weight gain on our aging bodies, but the weight of this world takes a far greater toll on our souls if we stay determined to carry it.

If you want a fire to last, you must kindle it. This means time spent in God's Word, time spent with other believers in fellowship and community, and time spent in corporate worship. Our ability to light this planet on fire for Jesus is only limited by our availability to Him. Throughout Scripture and three times in the book of Matthew alone, Jesus instructs us to pray, ask, seek, and knock. Matthew 6:33 reminds us, "But seek first the kingdom of God and his righteousness, and all these things will be added to you" (ESV).

More birthday candles help us shine even brighter for God's purpose.

One of the most common complaints people have as they age is that they're overlooked. Aging, they say, makes you invisible. Seems that adding some fire may remedy that grievance. God used fire to get His people's attention. Remember Moses and the burning bush or the pillar of fire the Israelites followed? Perhaps it's our turn to add a little fire to get the world to notice who He is. Fire is both hard to ignore and underestimate.

Today I can be grateful that my fire for the Lord can grow hotter as I age. More birthday candles help us shine even brighter for God's purpose. I can celebrate because I may be the perfect age to accomplish exactly what He created me for.

Prayer

Dear Heavenly Father, set me on fire anew for you. Kindle my love and passion for you. Help me, as I age, to never let that fire burn out but to fuel the flames so it can burn even brighter. Keep my soul and mind healthy by keeping them focused on things above rather than the frivolous pursuits vying to distract me from you.

Aging Gratefully in Action

How do you revive your fire for the Lord? It's about worship. Turn off the shows filled with bad news and celebrity gossip. Be intentional about what you're watching, reading, and scrolling past. Most of what culture offers by way of entertainment can distract and dampen our passion for the things of the Lord. Instead, keep your heart and mind fixed on things above (Colossians 3:2). Turn up the worship music, spend time in God's Word rather than online, and watch your fire for God grow. Through praise, worship, and intentionality we kindle the flame that allows us to burn brightly for our King.

Not Done Yet

*God's Promise of Abundant Life
Is Not Just for the Young*

The thief comes only to steal and kill and destroy; I have
come that they may have life and have it to the full.
JOHN 10:10

A re you living, or are you just alive? Numerous songs
and prose have posed this question. But as I think
about growing older, I can't help but come back to
it. Abundant life is more than just having a pulse—it's about
thriving with purpose. I love how the late Scottish author and
minister George MacDonald said, "Age is not all decay; it is the
ripening, the swelling of the fresh life within, that withers and
bursts the husks."[27]

   In Greek there are two words for life. There's your *bios* life—
your physical life, or the state of not being dead. And then
there is your life, which is your zest. *Zóé* life means "full, abundant life." A rich life that brims with purpose, fulfillment, and

satisfaction. This is the sweet yellow corn bursting through its green casing. But *zóé* life is not possible unless it's lived in Christ.

If we concentrate primarily on what's happening to our external bodies as we age, we can feel discouraged. We believe the culture's teaching that what's most important is our physical health. Of course taking care of the bodies God gave us is a good idea. But if we become so focused on our *bios* that we miss our *zóé*, we've missed the reason for staying alive!

Let's look at John 1:1–5 to understand how Jesus truly is life.

> In the beginning was the Word, and the Word was with God, and the Word was God. He was in the beginning with God. All things were made through him, and without him was not any thing made that was made. In him was life, and the life was the light of men. The light shines in the darkness, and the darkness has not overcome it. (ESV)

This is the understanding we need to feel truly alive no matter our age. Abundant life is not just for the young. Abundant life is for anyone who has found where true life exists—that is, in Christ. The best news is: abundant life isn't a promise for heaven—it's a promise for now.

One of the most awkward things I tell women on my podcast is that aging is real. I say it to challenge them with this truth: if their life's goal is only to have a better body, they're missing out on the abundant life God has for them. If our greatest pursuit is anything of this earth—our bodies included—we will reach the end of life and watch it all wither like the grass (Psalm 37:2). True freedom isn't found in an "after" photo. It's found when we taste the sweetness of the abundant life God created us to live right now.

This abundant life comes when we see what the Holy Spirit is doing inside us. Regardless of what is happening in our gravity-sensitive bodies, God's joy, peace, and love can fill us like a helium balloon. Flourishing doesn't mean having a wrinkle-free body at sixty. Looking youthful on the outside means nothing if there are no blossoms on the inside.

True flourishing is about seeing the Holy Spirit's fruit in our lives. From Galatians 5:22–23, the list is beautiful: love, joy, peace, patience, kindness, goodness, faithfulness, gentleness, and self-control. Can you imagine how alive we'd all feel if these traits dominated our days? Doesn't anxiety, envy, depression, anger, strivings, and strife melt away when this fruit blooms?

This message is urgent. We don't have an endless amount of time. Yet aging isn't a thief. Growing old isn't about sulking toward your grave. There is one who would have you believe these things. He's out to steal, kill, and destroy. But Jesus has a different message.

John 10:10 tells us, "The thief comes only to steal and kill and destroy; I have come that they may have life, and have it to the full." Who does Jesus promise abundant life to? There's no age demographic specified. So why do we often act like the best part of life is behind us? Why do we join in culture's practical joke believing that "real life" happens before you marry, have children, or get a "real" job? That's not life—that's childhood.

Real life happens when you don't look at it as a game to be won but as a gift to be treasured. Real life begins when you are old enough to understand that there is no *zóé* life aside from Christ. Real life isn't about being productive and checking off lists but cultivating a life in the Spirit.

Likewise, real beauty is about growing in the fruit of the spirit. If you've been following Jesus for a while now, that fruit is ripening. Or perhaps it's so plump, juicy, and ready to be picked that it's leaping off the tree. This is the sweetest way to age.

When culture references "ageless beauty," it points to a

woman who doesn't appear to age physically. It's about looking younger. But if our focus stays on the mirror's opinion of our appearance, we miss the beauty of growing old. Aging is a gift to our sanctification. We're working through hormonal changes and pressing through life stages. Time has sanded our rough edges and sharpened our corners. The older we get, the more opportunity we have to grow to look more like Jesus. Feelings of frumpiness flee when Christlikeness becomes our goal.

> ### The older we get, the more opportunity we have to grow to look more like Jesus.

Today I can be grateful this is a midlife celebration, not a midlife crisis. God's promise of abundant life isn't just for the young—it's for all. Remember, you're not over the hill . . . you're halfway to perfect.

Prayer

Dear Heavenly Father, help me remember that real life is found in you. Grow the fruit of the spirit in my life so I can experience the abundant life you intended for me. Help me be as intentional about my zóé *life in you as I am about my* bios *life.*

Aging Gratefully in Action

Science shows that getting outside and into nature is a powerful way to improve your psychological, physical, and spiritual well-being as you age. While our screens deplete us of energy, being outside reduces stress and cortisol levels, helping us release muscle tension and stress. Spiritually speaking, walking among trees and plants or along majestic bodies of water reminds us of our God's power and creativity. As we walk or play outdoors, we can savor the truth that this same God created and knows us. The whole earth shows His handiwork—you and I included (Psalm 19:1). The same God who has cared for nature from the beginning of time will also care for me as I age. That's something for which we can all be grateful.

Notes

1. Kumar, Karthik, MBBS. "When Does Skin Begin to Age." Medicinenet online. July 1, 2021. https://www.medicinenet.com/when _does_skin_begin_to_age/article.htm.

2. Park, Alice. "Our Brains Begin to Slow Down at Age 24." *Time Magazine Online*. April 15, 2014. https://time.com/63500/brain -aging-at-24/.

3. C. S. Lewis, *The Weight of Glory and Other Addresses* (New York: Harper One, 1980), 26.

4. Antonia Hoyle, "Meet the Woman Who Says She Hasn't Smiled for Forty Years . . . so She Doesn't Get Wrinkles," *Daily Mail*, February 1, 2015, https://www.dailymail.co.uk/femail/article-2935632/Meet -woman-says-hasn-t-smiled-40-years-doesn-t-wrinkles.html.

5. "75% of Women Now Color Their Hair Compared to 7% in 1950," SouthFloridaReporter.com, October 1, 2017, https:// southfloridareporter.com/75-women-now-color-hair-compared -7-1950/.

6. WebMD Editorial Contributors, reviewed by Carmelita Swiner, "Which Area of the Brain Is Most Susceptible to Shrinkage as We Age?," WebMD, April 07, 2023, https://www.webmd.com/healthy -aging/which-area-of-the-brain-is-most-suscepitble-to-shrinkage-as -we-age.

7. Cherry, Kendra. "What Is Neuroplasticity?" VeryWellMind.com, Nov 8, 2022. https://www.verywellmind.com/what-is-brain-plasticity -2794886.

---

8. John Piper, excerpts from his sermon "Don't Waste Your Life: Seven Minutes That Moved a Generation," May 19, 2017, desiringGod, https://www.desiringgod.org/messages/boasting-only-in-the-cross/excerpts/dont-waste-your-life.

9. Tim Challies, "Learning for Forever," *Challies.com* (blog), April 1, 2016, challies.com/articles/learning-for-forever/.

10. Charles Spurgeon, as quoted in David Guzik, "Joel 2," *Enduring Word Bible Commentary*, accessed May 9, 2022, https://enduringword.com/bible-commentary/joel-2/.

11. "Loneliness and Social Isolation Linked to Serious Health Conditions," Centers for Disease Control and Prevention, accessed June 1, 2022, https://www.cdc.gov/aging/publications/features/lonely-older-adults.html.

12. Diana Bruk, "Science Says You're the Loneliest at These Three Ages in Your Life," *BestLife*, June 8, 2019, https://bestlifeonline.com/science-says-youre-the-loneliest-at-these-three-ages-in-your-life/.

13. Jeffrey A. Hall, "How Many Hours Does It Take to Make a Friend," *Sage Journals* 36, no. 4 (March 15, 2018), https://doi.org/10.1177/0265407518761225.

14. Jimmy Evans, "A Reality Wedding," *Marriage Today*, YouTube video, 2:54, accessed June 10, 2022, https://www.youtube.com/watch?v=Gpa8ENbMskQ.

15. "Grandparents Who Babysit Grandkids May Live Longer," Cleveland Clinic Newsroom, September 7, 2017, https://newsroom.clevelandclinic.org/2017/09/07/study-grandparents-who-babysit-grandkids-may-live-longer/.

16. L. Gregory Jones and Célestin Musekura, *Forgiving as We've Been Forgiven: Community Practices for Making Peace* (Downers Grove, IL: IVP Books, 2010), 86.

17. Jones and Musekura's book *Forgiving as We've Been Forgiven* would be a great read for continuing study on this topic.

18. Luther, Martin, 1483–1546, "95 Theses Against Indulgences (English text)," First thesis.

19. Vicki Peterson, "Why Trauma Survivors Shouldn't Think They Are 'Lazy,'" *The Mighty*, February 12, 2020, https://themighty.com/2020/02/lazy-exhausted-in-trauma-recovery/.

20. "Do vs. Done" is an evangelism tool created by CRU ministries. Find out more about how to use this illustration to share the gospel at https://www.cru.org/content/dam/cru/legacy/2012/01/dovsdone.pdf.

21. "The Holy Reason We Say 'Goodbye' and What to Say Instead," Dictionary.com, September 9, 2020, https://www.dictionary.com/e /why-do-we-say-goodbye/.

22. Paul David Tripp, "Getting Older Every Day," PaulTripp.com, September 8, 2021, https://www.paultripp.com/wednesdays-word/posts /getting-older-every-day.

23. Clare Ansberry, "What Is the Perfect Age," *Wall Street Journal*, January 13, 2018, https://www.wsj.com/articles/what-is-the-perfect -age-1515844860.

24. "Is Fifty the Perfect Age?," The Harris Poll #63, Cision PR Newswire, September 12, 2013, https://www.prnewswire.com/news-releases/is -fifty-the-perfect-age-223472531.html.

25. Andrew Steptoe, Angus Deaton, and Arthur A. Stone, "Subjective Wellbeing, Health, and Ageing," *Lancet*, reviewed at Pubmed.gov, November 6, 2014, https://pubmed.ncbi.nlm.nih.gov/25468152/.

26. Dalton Thomas and Joel Richardson, *Sheep among Wolves*, documentary directed by Dalton Thomas (Frontier Alliance International and Maranatha, 2019), https://www.faistudios.org/documentaries.

27. George MacDonald, *The Marquis of Lossie*, 2 vols. (Leipzig, Bernard Tauchnitz: 1877), 1:279. Ebook at: https://www.gutenberg.org/cache /epub/7174/pg7174 images.html#CHAPTER_XL.